A Teacher's Guide to the

BOOK OF GALATIANS

Lee M. Ahlstrom

DISPENSATIONAL
PUBLISHING HOUSE, INC.

Copyright © 2019 Lee M. Ahlstrom
Cover and Illustration: Leonardo Costa
Cover and Illustrations © 2019 DispensationalPublishing House, Inc.

All rights reserved. This book or any portion thereof may not be reproduced or used in any manner whatsoever without the express written permission of the publisher except for the use of brief quotations in a book review.

Scriptures quoted as KJV are taken from the KING JAMES VERSION (KJV).

Printed in the United States of America
First Edition, First Printing, 2019
ISBN: 978-1-945774-39-3

Dispensational Publishing House, Inc.
220 Paseo del Pueblo Norte Taos, NM 87571

www.dispensationalpublishing.com

This is a DPH Quick Print book. Our QuickPrint process allows us to get books to the market at a much quicker pace and lower cost than the full book publishing process. If you discover errors in this book, please contact the publisher so that these errors may be fully removed in future editions.

Ordering Information: Quantity sales. Special discounts are available on quantity purchases by churches, associations, and others. For details, contact the publisher at the address above.

Orders by U.S. trade bookstores and wholesalers. Please contact the publisher: Tel: (844) 321-4202

1 2 3 4 5 6 7 8 9 10

Dedication

Being a teacher of God's Word is an awesome responsibility, regardless of the age of the students. It takes hours upon hours of study and research to properly prepare to stand before a classroom for 60 minutes. But it's more than just knowledge and transferring information. Leading a class is also about facilitating a discussion among students who may have different backgrounds and different levels of maturity in Christ, different opinions on social issues and current events. It's about building community as well.

These notes are dedicated first and foremost to my family – my wife, Pattie, and my children Julia, Lauren, and Dash. They have sacrificed countless hours of family time to my studies. They've also held me to a high standard, which I've strived to meet. In truth, it's not easy to be motivated every week to teach, but they inspire me. Thank you for all of your support and love!

I'd also like to thank my Sunday School class at Katy's First Baptist Church in Katy, Texas. We have a rather unique set of personalities and experiences with adults ranging from their 20's to their 80's. It's led to rich discussions of a wide variety of topics. They keep me on my toes, asking great questions and causing me to revisit my assumptions. You're wonderful!

And speaking of questioning assumptions, I'd like to thank the original 'questioner,' Dr. Randy White, currently of First Baptist Church in Taos, New Mexico. I had always been a Dispensationalist, but Dr. White's teaching pushed me to really refine several important ideas that crystallized my position on Scripture. We need more people who question the assumptions!

Table of Contents

Introduction 1

Introduction to the Book of Galatians 7

Galatians Chapter 1 21

Galatians Chapter 2 37

Galatians Chapter 3 55

Galatians Chapter 4 81

Galatians Chapter 5 109

Galatians Chapter 6 139

Epilogue 165

INTRODUCTION

Why I've Written This Study

I've been teaching Sunday School classes and small groups for more than 15 years. When I began, I quickly realized that most of the denominational curricula were an inch deep. They're designed with the 'baby' Christian in mind. I understand the philosophy—keep everything at a basic level so that any visitor who comes to the class will have a lesson from which they can take an essential truth, i.e., "God is Love," "The Cross is Critical," etc. Unfortunately, if every lesson looks like this, Christians never mature. They never move from the milk to the meat (Heb. 5:12-14).

What was worse was that every quarter, the materials were written by different contributors on relatively short passages of scriptures. In other words, they might take a chapter (or three) of Exodus this week, then jump ten chapters and take two or three more. There's nothing wrong with that, but it does raise the issue of inconsistency. In particular, different contributors often have different hermeneutics, or approaches to interpreting Scripture. One contributor might take one approach to a passage or topic while another might take a very different and often contradictory approach. This leaves the teacher in a quandary—what's the right approach? It also allows commentators to skip over difficult passages. Again, that's fine if you want an easy Sunday School class, but not if you want to understand Scripture.

These notes are designed for the Christian ready for some meat. They are meant to be an expositional, verse-by-verse approach to Galatians designed to help the serious, committed student dig into God's Word.

My approach has some foundational precepts which I try to maintain:

- All Scripture is inspired (God-Breathed) by the Lord (2 Tim. 3:15).

- Words matter. Every word is there for a reason and we can learn a great deal by studying those words. In addition, the original language matters. Greek and Hebrew are both precise languages and words in these languages can be incredibly descriptive. Furthermore, our English translations don't tell us the full story—word meanings today don't necessarily coincide with the meanings of the translations we use in these lessons, the King James (based on the *Textus Receptus* (TR), or "Received Text"), so digging into the Greek or Hebrew often provides key insights.

- As mentioned above, we do use the King James in these notes. We are by no means in the 'King James-only' camp, as some of the more modern translations do a better job translating the ideas of *certain* verses, but overall, we believe the TR is a better foundation than the texts on which newer versions are based and in fact, believe there are serious issues with the Nestle-Aland (NA) Greek text (the basis of the NIV, ESV, etc.), compiled by theological liberals. As a homework assignment, we would recommend a study of how we got our Bible and a review of the differences between the TR and NA Greek texts.

- Let Scripture Interpret Scripture. The Bible is consistent in its use of idioms, symbolism, etc. For example, I believe leaven is *always* a type or symbol of sin. We do subscribe to the 'Law/Principle of First Mention'—that is, when something is first mentioned as a symbol in Scripture, future references can be interpreted to be consistent. For example, birds are first mentioned in Genesis 40:17 where Joseph is interpreting the dream of the baker in prison. They are obviously symbolic and are an evil omen because the baker is going to die. We can't ignore context. Sometimes a bird is just a bird. But when we look at passages which are clearly symbolic, the key is *consistency*. For example, when we get to Matthew 13 and Jesus describes the Kingdom as having grown so large as to shelter the birds of the air, is this a good thing or a bad thing? I'll suggest that under the Law of First Mention, it's a *bad* thing—and that changes your view of the passage completely!

- "If the literal sense makes sense, seek no other sense, lest you end up with nonsense." We take the Bible literally (see 'words matter'). This doesn't mean that we don't allow for figures of speech in Scripture. E.W. Bullinger's "Figures of Speech Used in the Bible" categorizes more than 200 different types including similes, metaphors, etc. These are fairly easy to spot. Psalm 91 says that under God's *"wings shalt thou trust."* Do we think God really has wings? Of course not—it's a figure of speech. *However*, let us not be quick to throw everything in the figure-of-speech-camp. When Christ or

Paul speak of the Kingdom of God, there is **every evidence that the Kingdom is real, physical, and future.** It is not some allegorical 'kingdom in your heart' or a kingdom that is 'already, but not yet.' You do yourself (and your students) a disservice by failing to grasp this critical concept.

- Finally, and certainly not least importantly, our study takes a Dispensational approach to Scripture. God deals with man in different ways at different times throughout Scripture. These are *not* inconsistent—rather the Lord revealed Himself to man through progressive revelation. He dealt with Adam one way, long before the Law was instituted. He dealt with Jews under the period of the Law. Today, Believers are fortunate enough to live in an age of Grace in which He no longer requires animal sacrifices. Law and Grace are incompatible—a key concept in Galatians. But don't make the mistake of thinking that God is done with Israel—He has a plan that has been foretold since Genesis. The Jews are His people and He will redeem them. All of this to say, if you come from a Reformed perspective, I'm pleased you're here and I pray that you find this resource useful, but it will challenge most, if not all, of the tenants of your hermeneutic.

How to Use These Notes

When I teach a class, I tend to use the Socratic method. My goal is to stimulate conversation, not to lecture. Galatians, however, is a bit tough in this respect. In the early chapters, there tends to a bit more lecture. However, as we hit chapters 5 and 6, there was quite a bit more discussion as I taught.

I would recommend you start by reading the entire letter to the Galatians. Understand the key issue—law vs. grace—and get to know the flow of Paul's argument that grace is superior. It will help as you teach to understand how the letter is structured—Chapters 1 and 2 are focused on Paul's credentials; Chapters 3 and 4 are doctrinal; Chapters 5 and 6 are personal.

The notes take the letter in bite-sized chunks, largely defined by the headers we find in the New King James Version. However, for a variety of reasons, we quote the King James Version in these notes. What's important for you to remember is that the section breaks we've used are arbitrary. Paul did not write his letters with chapter and verse numbers. His thoughts flowed freely throughout the text just the way our own letters do. Thus, it's sometimes the case that a thought or argument might carry over between sections.

Each chapter has an introduction, the lesson, and a conclusion. It's really to help the teacher guide the time in the classroom. You should, of course, feel free to alter those to fit your own style/personality and that of your class or small group.

It took me about 16 weeks to teach the entire book, but you should go at your own pace dictated entirely dependent on your style and the participation from your class. Don't worry about stopping in the middle of the chapter-just be sure to summarize where you are at the beginning of the following class. Remember, you may have guests and it's always worthwhile to summarize the big ideas of the book or section at the beginning of the lessons.

I've tried to write the notes in a conversational manner, asking questions and then answering them. How much discussion you want to encourage is up to you.

A Final Word

I've compiled these notes using a variety of sources. I use Logos Bible software and am fortunate to have a pretty extensive library. Feel free, however, to supplement the notes with your own resources.

However, I offer one caveat. Many resources you find online or in your own library will not be fully compatible with these notes. As I said, I am approaching this from a Dispensational hermeneutic. This means that if you open a commentary by a Reformed pastor (a Sproul, Calvin, or Luther), there are passages where we will completely disagree. Specifically those involving Israel, the Elect, and the Church. Thus, as you look at other resources, do so with a critical eye to see whether they fit with this approach.

Finally, your job as a teacher and the responsibility of your students is found in Acts 17:11:

> *These were more noble than those in Thessalonica, in that they received the word with all readiness of mind, and searched the scriptures daily, whether those things were so.*

Don't take what's written here as 'gospel.' I've done my best to write a comprehensive set of notes that I believe will be useful to teachers and students alike. I have tried to maintain internal consistency in my approach and tried to answer questions/arguments that I think might arise during a discussion. Nevertheless, no one is perfect, so if you find inconsistencies or errors, please correct them for the sake of your students. And if this work helps you teach God's Word, I am eternally grateful.

Lee Ahlstrom, July 2019

INTRODUCTION TO THE BOOK OF GALATIANS

INTRODUCTION

- As we enter our study of Galatians, we're going to tackle one of the New Testament books that has direct applicability to Christians in the Church Age.
  - Of course, Paul's letter to Timothy tells us that *"For whatsoever things were written aforetime were written for our learning, that we through patience and comfort of the scriptures might have hope"* (Rom. 15:4).
  - Dispensationally, not everything in the Bible applies to the Church. In the Old Testament, for example, the Jews were under the Law. We Christians are not.
- But Paul's writings are directly applicable to us and Galatians is one of Paul's key letters. In the Book, Paul will:
  - Defend his credentials as an apostle and the authenticity of the Gospel he preached;

- Explain how Grace is superior to Law and decry the "Judaizers," the legalistic Jews who sought to impose burdens on Jewish and Gentile converts to Christianity; and
- Instruct how to live a life of Christian liberty.

➤ Galatians has been a key book since its writing:
- Many authors cite the idea that Galatians is the "Magna Carta of Christian Liberty."[1]
- It was a key book for Martin Luther at the time of the Reformation: "Luther especially loved it. He called it his Catherine von Bora, for, he said, 'I am wedded to it.' In Luther's hands the book became a mighty weapon in the Reformation arsenal."[2]
  - The words he wrote in the preface to his 1535 commentary still ring true today:

    > This doctrine can never be discussed and taught enough. If it is lost and perishes, the whole knowledge of truth, life, and salvation is lost and perishes at the same time. But if it flourishes, everything good flourishes – religion, true worship, the glory of God, and the right knowledge of all things and of all social conditions. There is clear and present danger that the devil may take away from us the pure doctrine of faith and may substitute for it the doctrines of works and of human traditions. It is very necessary, therefore, that this doctrine of faith be continually read and heard in public.[3]

  - In fact, one of the key verses that brought Luther to the

---

1 This phrase is frequently claimed and quoted (cf., introduction by James Boice in *The Expositor's Bible Commentary* and multiple other citations). However, I am unable to determine the originator of the phrase. Still, it seems appropriate.

2 Boice, J. M. (1976). Galatians. In F. E. Gaebelein (Ed.), *The Expositor's Bible Commentary: Vol. 10. Romans through Galatians* (p. 409). Grand Rapids, MI: Zondervan Publishing House.

3 George, T. (1994). *Galatians: Vol. 30* (pp. 69-70). Nashville: Broadman & Holman Publishers.

point of challenging the Catholic church was his reading of Habakkuk 2:4, *"The Just shall live by faith,"* and a realization that this verse forms the foundation of a trilogy of letters in the New Testament:

- Romans – describes 'the Just'
- Galatians – describes how 'to Live'
- Hebrews – is about 'Faith'

- It's sometimes known as "a short Romans." Whereas Paul defines and defends the gospel with his head in Romans, he does so with his heart in Galatians.
- R. Longenecker, in his commentary, *Galatians*, states that the letter is "like a lion turned loose in the arena of Christianity."[4]

LESSON

> Let's talk a bit about who wrote Galatians. It's important to understand the background of our author as we examine his writings.
  - It is widely accepted that Paul is the author. Why?
    - He refers to himself in the opening (Galatians 1:1).
    - He gives a personal biography about key details in his life and ministry (Galatians 1:10-2:5).
    - He claims to have signed the letter in his own hand (Galatians 6:11).
  - What are some facts about Paul? How much do you know about him?
    - Born in Tarsus to a Jewish mother and Roman father

---

4 Ibid, 22.

- Named Saul; later went by Paul
- Roman citizen (through his father)
- Studied under Gamaliel, one of the most respected Jewish rabbis
- Was a tentmaker
- A 'Pharisee of the Pharisees'
- Was a harsh persecutor of the early church
- Converted on Road to Damascus; blinded; cured
- Suffered from a thorn in the side from which he never recovered
- Spent three years in Arabia
- Three missionary journeys
- Stoned and left for dead
- Disputed doctrine with Peter
- Wrote most of the New Testament [11 (or 12 if we count Hebrews) of the 28 letters - counting Christ's letters to the 7 Churches]
- Shipwrecked and bitten by an asp
- Brought to trials in Jerusalem and Rome
- Presumably executed by Nero

- Let's look at a few key events for Paul:
  - We're introduced to Saul of Tarsus in the first verse of Acts 8 – *"Now Saul was consenting to his death."*
    - Whose death? Stephen.
    - And why was Stephen killed? Because he preached that

Jesus was the Jewish Messiah.

- Important to recognize as we look at Acts that up through at least chapter 9, it is the Kingdom Gospel being preached to Jews by the Jewish disciples and apostles. The church is still a mystery. Look at Peter's sermon and how it's described and who the audience is. Look at Stephen's testimony before the Sanhedrin.

○ Paul is converted in Acts 9. Key events include:

- Paul's persecution of those who were of the Way – Jews! – who would be bound and brought to Jerusalem
- Paul sees a bright light and falls to the ground
- He hears the voice of Christ, but the others with him only hear thunder
- He is blinded and led by the hand to Ananias in Damascus
- His sight is restored
- Spends days with the disciples and immediately begins preaching Jesus is the Son of God. But where does he do this? In Synagogues. In fact, as we look at the pattern of Paul, even on his journeys, he always starts in synagogues because his heart is for his people. It's not until Acts 18 when Paul finally turns away from the Jews and says, *"Your blood be upon your own heads. I am clean. From now on I will go to the Gentiles"* (Acts 18:6). But he still has a heart for his people as shown in Romans 9-11.

○ A key event occurs when Paul shows up in Jerusalem in Acts 15 that is actually critical in helping us understand the book of Galatians. Let's review Acts 15:1-5:

> *1 And certain men came down from Judea and taught the brethren, "Unless you are circumcised according to the custom of Moses, you cannot be saved." 2 Therefore, when Paul and Barnabas had no small dissension and dispute with them, they determined that Paul and Barnabas and certain others of them should go up to Jerusalem, to the apostles and elders, about this question.*
>
> *3 So, being sent on their way by the church, they passed through Phoenicia and Samaria, describing the conversion of the Gentiles; and they caused great joy to all the brethren. 4 And when they had come to Jerusalem, they were received by the church and the apostles and the elders; and they reported all things that God had done with them. 5 But some of the sect of the Pharisees who believed rose up, saying, "It is necessary to circumcise them, and to command them to keep the law of Moses."*

- What's the key issue here? It's that *"certain men"* from Judea are teaching that the Law of Moses must be followed or one *"cannot be saved"* (Acts 15:1).

- Yet Paul and Barnabas dispute this vigorously and end up going to Jerusalem to settle the matter. See Acts 15:6-11 – The Jerusalem Counsel:

> *6 And the apostles and elders came together for to consider of this matter. 7 And when there had been much disputing, Peter rose up, and said unto them, Men and brethren, ye know how that a good while ago God made choice among us, that the Gentiles by my mouth should hear the word of the gospel, and believe. 8 And God, which knoweth the hearts, bare them witness, giving them the Holy Ghost, even as he did unto us; 9 And put no difference between us and them, purifying their hearts by faith. 10 Now therefore why tempt ye God, to put a yoke upon the neck of the disciples, which neither our fathers nor we were able to bear? 11 But we believe that through the grace of the Lord Jesus Christ we shall be saved, even as they.*

- Notice how Peter responds as Acts 15 continues. He does not dispute Paul and Barnabas – rather look at his words:

"we shall be saved in the same manner as they" (the Gentiles) (Acts 15:11).

- Think about that. Peter doesn't say the Gentiles will be saved like the Jews, rather it's the reverse! The Jews will be saved like the Gentiles – through faith. Let's read Acts 15:12-21:

  > *12 Then all the multitude kept silence, and gave audience to Barnabas and Paul, declaring what miracles and wonders God had wrought among the Gentiles by them.*
  >
  > *13 And after they had held their peace, James answered, saying, Men and brethren, hearken unto me: 14 Simeon hath declared how God at the first did visit the Gentiles, to take out of them a people for his name. 15 And to this agree the words of the prophets; as it is written,*
  >
  > *16 After this I will return, and will build again the tabernacle of David, which is fallen down; and I will build again the ruins thereof, and I will set it up: 17 That the residue of men might seek after the Lord, and all the Gentiles, upon whom my name is called, saith the Lord, who doeth all these things.*
  >
  > *18 Known unto God are all his works from the beginning of the world. 19 Wherefore my sentence is, that we trouble not them, which from among the Gentiles are turned to God: 20 But that we write unto them, that they abstain from pollutions of idols, and from fornication, and from things strangled, and from blood. 21 For Moses of old time hath in every city them that preach him, being read in the synagogues every sabbath day.*

- So, the Counsel ends up sending forth a decree declaring that the Gentiles should abstain from a few things, but in no way follow the Law of Moses.
- This is a critical point to remember as we look into Galatians.

➤ Let's discuss a bit about Galatia and the Galatians:
- Galatia was part of what we now call Turkey.

- The region was named after the Gaulic or Celtic people who ultimately settled there.
- The Celts first appeared in history as a distinct ethnic or people group sometime around 500 BC. when they occupied the Danube River basin in central Europe. They were known for their bravery in battle and for their restless spirit. From their Germanic base they spread out into the various extremities of the European mainland. Some of them settled in what is today France, giving the name Gaul to that country.[5] Others migrated to the British Isles, where their form of life took root in the Celtic culture of Ireland and the Gaelic dialect of the Highland Scots. Other groups of Celts spread southeastward into the Balkan peninsula and from there into Asia Minor.[6] This region came to be known as North Galatia.
- The Celts established themselves there as an independent kingdom until around 25 BC when Augustus Caesar created a Roman territory. This territory included Pamphylia, Lystra, Derbe, et. al. Thus, by the time of Paul's journeys, Galatia stretched from the Mediterranean Sea to the Black Sea across Asia Minor.
- Thus, there were actually two areas that were referred to as Galatia – the original Northern region and the Southern Roman province.
    - Scholars debate to whom this letter was written. Not terribly important from our point of view, but there appears to be little evidence that Paul visited the Northern region while his missionary journeys certainly placed him in Lystra, Iconium, and Derbe.

---

5 cf. Julius Caesar's commentaries on the Gallic War
6 George, *Galatians*, 39

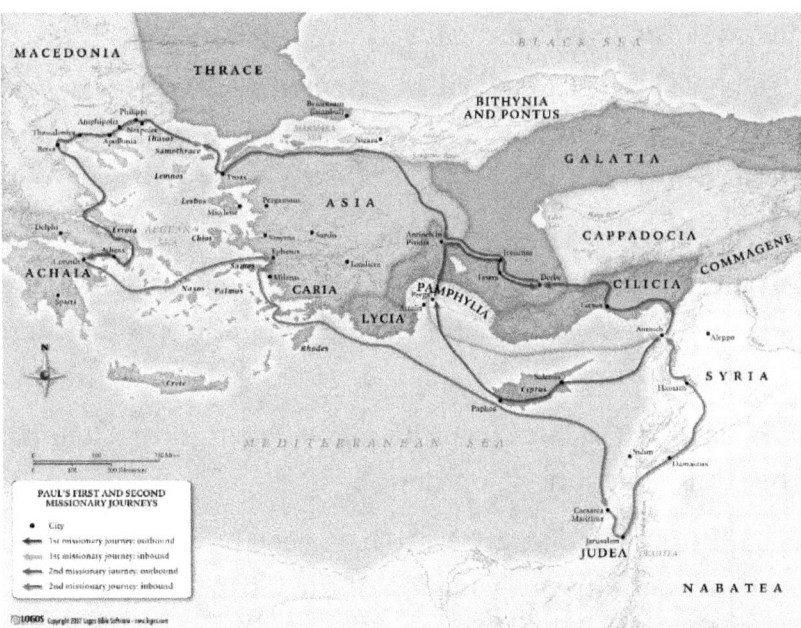

- The original inhabitants of north Galatia were Phrygians, many of whom still remained in the 1st century AD, together with some Greeks and a fairly large community of Jews. Although the area was cosmopolitan, the Celtic element predominated. These people were known for their sturdy independence, but also for their drunkenness and reveling. They were of an inquisitive disposition and were easily impressed with new ideas, particularly of a religious kind. They were nevertheless easily turned aside and had a reputation for fickleness. In religious matters there is evidence that they were highly superstitious and were especially attracted to the wild rites of the goddess Cybele. It is not difficult to imagine the impact the Christian gospel may have made on a people of such temperament. Paul's letter to the Galatians reflects several of the traits of the Gallic peoples.[7]

---

[7] Guthrie, D. (1988). Galatia. In *Baker Encyclopedia of the Bible: Vol. 1* (p. 829). Grand Rapids, MI: Baker Book House.

- Timing of the letter
  - There are at least two views of when Galatians was written, though it seems generally agreed that it was among the first letters.
  - An early view dates it at some time around AD 49-50. This would be just before Acts 15 Council of Jerusalem, but after his First Missionary Journey and the founding of the churches on that Journey.
  - The later date places it in the mid-50's, after the Council and his Third Missionary Journey.
  - In either case, it does appear to have been before Romans, which is Paul's definitive explanation of the Gospel of Grace, written sometime around AD 57.
- The letter is broken up into three segments
  - Biographical – Chapters 1 and 2
  - Doctrinal – Chapters 3 and 4
  - Practical – Chapters 5 and 6
- Finally, there are some unique characteristics of this letter among all of Paul's other letters.
  - It is a stern letter, with no commendation to the readers, no praise, no thanksgiving.
  - There is no request for prayer and no mention of the Galatians' standing in Christ.
  - He mentions no one traveling with him.

CONCLUSION

Next to Romans, Galatians is one of the most important NT letters from which the modern church should draw its doctrine. If there is any doubt about whether we are under the Law or need to add anything other than belief in Christ as our Savior in order to be justified, Galatians should disabuse us of that idea.

Timeline of Paul's Life
(all dates approximate)

Date	Activity
4 – 10 AD	Birth of Paul in Tarsus as a Roman citizen - Acts 22 Paul's education under Gamaliel and as a tentmaker
~30 – 33 AD	Ministry of Jesus
~33 AD	Crucifixion of Jesus
~34 AD	Martyrdom of Stephen; Paul a participant - Acts 9
~34 AD	Paul's journey to Damascus; Conversion - Acts 9
~37 – 40 AD	Paul preaches in **SYNAGOGUES** in Damascus; Spends 3 years in Arabia before returning to Damascus Acts 9:19-22; Galatians 1:15-17
~40 AD	Forced to flee in a basket - Acts 9:25
~40 AD	First visit to Jerusalem; Introduced by Barnabas-other disciples suspicious; Stays 15 days, smuggled out to Caesarea, then Tarsus - Acts 9:26-30; Galatians 1:18-20
~44 AD	Herod dies - Acts 12
~46 D	Brief visit to Jerusalem to bring food to the Jerusalem church; First Missionary Journey begins-Salamis, Paphos, Antioch (Pisidia), Iconium, Lystra, Derbe - Acts 13,14
~49 – 50 AD	**Paul writes the Letter to the Galatians (earlier date)**
~50 – 51 AD	Return to Jerusalem 14 years after first visit bringing with him Barnabas and Titus; Conference of Acts 15 - Galatians 1:21 - 2:1; Acts 15

Timeline of Paul's Life Continued
(all dates approximate)

Date	Activity
50 – 51 AD	Second Missionary Journey: Philippi, Thessalonica, Berea, Athens, Corinth, Ephesus; Barnabas departs with John Mark; Paul moves on with Titus; Return to Antioch - Acts 15 – 18
~50 – 51 AD	**Paul writes 1st and 2nd Thessalonians**
~52 – 57 AD	Third Missionary Journey: Galatia, Ephesus, 2nd visit to Corinth, Philippi, Troas, Patara, Tyre, back to Jerusalem - Acts 18 – 21
~53 – 56 AD	Paul in Ephesus; Nero succeeds Claudius (53 AD)
~55 – 56 AD	**Paul writes the Letter to the Galatians (later date)**
~56 AD	**Paul writes 1st and 2nd Corinthians**
~57 AD	Arrested in Jerusalem; Accused before the Sanhedrin; Sent under guard to Governor Felix at Caesarea - Acts 21 – 24
~57 AD	**Paul writes Romans**
~59 AD	Festus succeeds Felix; Trials before Festus and Agrippa; Paul appeals to Rome - Acts 25 – 26
~60 AD	Departure for Rome; Shipwrecked on Malta where they winter; Arrival and house arrest in Rome - Acts 27 – 28
~60 AD	**Paul writes Philemon, Ephesians, Colossians, Philippians, Titus, 1st and 2nd Timothy, Hebrews (?)**
~62 AD	Release in Rome; Visit to Asia
~64 – 68 AD	Re-arrest; Execution

GALATIANS CHAPTER 1

INTRODUCTION

➤ Last week, we completed our introduction to the Epistle to the Galatians. We learned:
- Paul was its author—we'll talk a little more about that today.
- Galatia was a region that we would today identify as the middle of Turkey running from the Mediterranean to the Black Sea.
- The inhabitants were of Celtic descent, having migrated across Europe and settled there before the birth of Christ. They were a fickle and warlike people, easily given to new ideas.
- There were two Galatias-a Northern (which had been the old, independent kingdom of Galatia) and the Southern, a Roman province. Paul is *probably* writing to the churches in Southern part of Galatia which included Iconium, Derbe, and Lystra.
- It's not entirely clear when the letter was written—there is an early date which places it in the late 40's making it one of Paul's first letters, and a late date of the mid-50's, which is still early among Paul's writings, but after several other letters had been written.

- ➤ We discussed the importance of the letter and how it has been referred to as the "Magna Carta" or "Declaration of Independence" for Christian liberty, and its importance in the Reformation, particularly to Martin Luther, and how it forms part of the New Testament trilogy of Galatians, Romans, and Hebrews based on Habakkuk 2:4, *"The Just shall live by faith."*
- ➤ The letter is divided into 3 parts
  - Chapters 1 and 2 are biographical, about Paul
  - Chapter 3 and 4 are doctrinal
  - Chapter 5 and 6 are practical
- ➤ Let's move into Chapter 1, and as a brief exercise, let's assume you were applying for a job and you were writing to your potential employer. What would you want him/her to know?
  - Your qualifications
  - Your education
  - Your previous work history
  - Your character
  - Your references
- ➤ As we read Chapters 1 and 2, we're going to find that Paul will give us all of these things and he'll do this to establish his authority to correct some fundamentally dangerous teachings that have crept into the Galatian churches from Judaizers, Jews who believed and taught that Gentiles had to first become Jews in order to be saved.
  - Some of this may be have sincere error. Remember that there is no concept in the Jewish mind of the church and the idea of salvation by trusting in Jesus. Jesus was Jewish, He followed the Law, you had to go through Jesus. Thus, it may have made

logical sense to the Jewish mind that you had to become Jewish first. We should not assume a nefarious motive *a priori*.

- On the other hand, there may have been something darker going on here. An attempt by the Judaizers to assert their superiority over the new converts and keep their place at the top of God's social structure.
    - As we'll see, Paul is going to react incredibly strongly to that and in doing so, give us the freedom to be who we are in Christ.

LESSON

 Galatians 1:1-5

> *1 Paul, an apostle, (not of men, neither by man, but by Jesus Christ, and God the Father, who raised him from the dead;) 2 And all the brethren which are with me, unto the churches of Galatia: 3 Grace be to you and peace from God the Father, and from our Lord Jesus Christ, 4 Who gave himself for our sins, that he might deliver us from this present evil world, according to the will of God and our Father: 5 To whom be glory for ever and ever. Amen.*

> Paul jumps right into the heart of the matter. How does he describe himself?

- As an "apostle." What is the definition of an 'apostle?'
    - **Apostle** – ἀπόστολος *apóstolos*; genitive. *apostólou*, masculine noun from *apostéllō* (649), to send. Used as a [substitute], one sent, apostle, ambassador[8]

---

[8] Zodhiates, S. (2000). *The complete word study dictionary: New Testament* (electronic ed.). Chattanooga, TN: AMG Publishers.

- And if one is sent or is serving as an ambassador, we need to ask, "Whose ambassador is he? *Who* sent him?" We will discuss that in a moment.
- But another point we should make here is that the ambassador serving the one sent has spent time with the one sending. How else can he properly convey the wishes or instructions of the one who sent him or her?
- How many apostles were there?
  - Originally, there were only the twelve. When used in the Gospels, it refers to this circle (Mark 3:14; Luke 6:13).
  - Matthias was selected by lot in Acts 1 to replace Judas Iscariot
  - However, Acts 14:14 also refers to Barnabas and Paul as apostles.
  - Paul counts James (Jesus' brother) as an Apostle in Galatians 1:19. Though not a believer at the time of Jesus' death, 1 Corinthians 15:7 says Jesus appeared to James and gave him instructions
  - Jesus is also called *"the Apostle and High Priest of our confession"* in Hebrews 3:1.
  - In general, the point is that there do not appear to be a large number of apostles.
- How do this differ from a disciple?
  - A disciple is a general student or pupil who followed a religious leader. For example, Mark 2:18 mentions disciples of John the Baptist while John 9:28 talks about disciples of Moses.
  - The Gospels sometimes refer to the Twelve as 'disciples,' which is still accurate.

- Jesus' disciples included many who were not part of the Twelve and many women (Mary, Martha, Mary Magdalene, etc.).
- We **ARE** disciples of Christ as well. We seek to understand more about Him and His teachings and to enjoy the special relationship available to those who believed on Him for salvation.
- We **ARE NOT** apostles. You may sometimes see independent churches that have billboards claiming that "Apostle So-and-So" is the leader of that congregation. Be wary. If they have that wrong, chances are there will be other doctrinal issues.

- So, Paul has made a claim to be an apostle. Who sent him? This is important as he establishes his credentials.
  - Two negatives:
    - Not from men – No man had sent Paul to the Galatian churches.
    - Not through men – No one had ordained Paul as an Apostle – not Peter, James, John, etc.
  - Instead, it is none other than Jesus Christ and God the Father (who raised Christ from the Dead) who have put Paul on this mission
    - That's a strong set of credentials. This is not some junior deputy under-ambassador who was sent on by the senior deputy under-ambassador. Paul is making the claim that he has received his authority from Christ.
    - What does that mean for his readers? Paul had the authority to back up his words, so they needed to take heed.

- Paul also acknowledges the others who are with him to the churches or assemblies as he brings the Galatians a characteristic greeting:
  - **Grace** – χάρις *cháris*; genitive. *cháritos*, feminine noun from *chaírō* (5463), to rejoice. Grace, particularly that which causes joy, pleasure, gratification, favor, acceptance, for a kindness granted or desired, a benefit, thanks, gratitude.[9]
  - Grace (*charis*) is closely related to the common Greek word for "hello" (*chaire*).[10]
  - Thus 'grace' was a common greeting among the Gentiles.
  - **Peace** – εἰρήνη *eirḗnē*; genitive. *eirḗnēs*, feminine noun. Peace. **(I)** Particularly in a single sense, the opposite of war and dissension (Luke 14:32; Acts 12:20; Rev. 6:4). Among individuals, peace, harmony (Matt. 10:34; Luke 12:51; Acts 7:26; Rom. 14:19). In Hebrews 7:2, *"King of peace,"* means a peaceful king. Metaphorically peace of mind, tranquility, arising from reconciliation with God and a sense of a divine favor (Rom. 5:1; 15:13; Phil. 4:7 [cf. Is. 53:5]).[11]
  - This was the Greek equivalent of the Hebrew *shalom*.
  - So perhaps we are seeing a greeting that resonates with both the Gentiles and the Jews in the congregation.
  - Paul began all of his letters with this characteristic greeting.
  - It is interesting that he greets them in Grace but will question them about their lack of grace and adherence to the Law.
- Where does this grace and peace come from? It comes from God the Father, but also from Jesus.

---

9 Ibid.

10 George, *Galatians*, 85.

11 Zodhiates, *The complete word study dictionary: New Testament*.

- ▸ Here Paul describes what Jesus has done for us.
  - We can also refer to Paul's telling of the gospel of salvation in 1 Corinthians 15:1-11 – the 'what' of the Gospel:

    > *15 Moreover, brethren, I declare unto you the gospel which I preached unto you, which also ye have received, and wherein ye stand; 2 By which also ye are saved, if ye keep in memory what I preached unto you, unless ye have believed in vain. 3 For I delivered unto you first of all that which I also received, how that Christ died for our sins according to the scriptures; 4 And that he was buried, and that he rose again the third day according to the scriptures: 5 And that he was seen of Cephas, then of the twelve: 6 After that, he was seen of above five hundred brethren at once; of whom the greater part remain unto this present, but some are fallen asleep. 7 After that, he was seen of James; then of all the apostles. 8 And last of all he was seen of me also, as of one born out of due time. 9 For I am the least of the apostles, that am not meet to be called an apostle, because I persecuted the church of God. 10 But by the grace of God I am what I am: and his grace which was bestowed upon me was not in vain; but I laboured more abundantly than they all: yet not I, but the grace of God which was with me. 11 Therefore whether it were I or they, so we preach, and so ye believed.*

  - We always need to include the Resurrection in our telling of the gospel. We often focus on the cross, which is true and good, but if we miss the Resurrection, we miss the deliverance from death that the cross achieved.

  - Paul's introductory verses in Galatians are an excellent corollary to 1st Corinthians 15 because they tell us the *'why:'*
    - "*that He might deliver us from this present evil age*" (Galatians 1:4).
    - The idea of deliverance here is to 'take or pluck out' out of the current time of evil (which is derived from labor, toil, sorrow).

- - So, what does this mean? We know we will be delivered from a future age of evil (the Tribulation), but how are we delivered from this age?
    - We're certainly still a part of this world, aren't we? We experience all the pain and sorrow this world has to offer. We, and those around us, suffer from our own sin and the sins of the rest of the world.
    - Yet, we do not have to live controlled by sin. Paul tells us in Romans that we are to throw off that 'old man' of sin and live as a new man.
    - Thus, we are delivered into the ability to do that through the Holy Spirit. Though we often fail to take advantage of that 'super-power.'

> Paul concludes his greeting with a doxology. If Jesus sacrificed Himself for our sins and delivered us to a new life in Him, how could both He and the Father not be afforded GLORY forever and ever!

 Galatians 1:6-10

6 I marvel that ye are so soon removed from him that called you into the grace of Christ unto another gospel: 7 Which is not another; but there be some that trouble you, and would pervert the gospel of Christ. 8 But though we, or an angel from heaven, preach any other gospel unto you than that which we have preached unto you, let him be accursed. 9 As we said before, so say I now again, If any man preach any other gospel unto you than that ye have received, let him be accursed. 10 For do I now persuade men, or God? or do I seek to please men? for if I yet pleased men, I should not be the servant of Christ.

- ➤ Now that the niceties are out of the way, Paul moves right into the key issue. They are perverting the gospel.
  - Paul 'wonders' or 'is struck with astonishment' that the Galatians have turned away so quickly from what he had taught them about the gospel. As we read further, consider that this gives us some insight into what Paul had taught churches as he was forming them.
  - The fact that they turned away quickly to another gospel is perfectly illustrative of the fickle nature of the Gauls/Celts.
    - The Greek word for 'quickly' is *tacheos* and is used to describe an event that, when it occurs, occurs quickly. This is not saying that the event occurs soon but that it unfolds rapidly. Look for the word in the book of Revelation.
  - But it also highlights the need for *ongoing* discipleship. We cannot simply lead someone to Christ, give ourselves a pat on the back and our convert a pat on the head and send him on his way. We must disciple. We must direct them on the paths of righteousness lest they wander away. I think this is where we fall short as God's people and God's church.
  - Literally, the Galatians are being displaced from one place to another, changing sides. They are forsaking the *grace* (there's that word again) of Christ, which delivered them, for something else.

- ➤ What have they turned to?
  - "*another gospel: Which is not another*" – What does this mean?
    - There are two words for 'another' in Greek; both are used here.
      - *Heteros* – another of a different kind. Heterogenous materials are made up of different kinds of substances.

- *Allos* – another of the same kind
- If I hold up my mechanical pencil and say, "It's broken. Can you bring me another?" and you bring me the exact same pencil, you've brought me an *allos*. But if you bring me a yellow #2, you've brought me a *heteros*. You don't see that in the English, but it's clear in the Greek.
  - They have turned away to a 'different' gospel – a *heteros* gospel – that is not 'another' – an *allos* gospel. And as it turns out, this new 'gospel' or 'good news' isn't really good news at all!

➤ The worst part of all of this is that this is being done on purpose.
- Paul says there are some who "*would*" – in Greek, this expresses a desire, an act of choice.
- Who are these people? The Judaizers!

➤ And now Paul gives a warning that if anyone, even an angel from Heaven (Mormons anyone?) should come preaching a pervasion of the gospel he preached (evangelized), they are to be anathema.
- **Anathema** – ἀνάθεμα anáthema; genitive. anathématos, neutral noun from **anatíthēmi** (394), to place, lay up. A gift given by vow or in fulfillment of a promise, and given up or devoted to destruction for God's sake (Sept.: Num. 21:1–3; Deut. 13:16–18); therefore, given up to the curse and destruction, accursed (1 Cor. 12:3; 16:22; Gal. 1:8, 9).[12]
- That's serious. And Paul is serious. He repeats the warning in verse 9. So, there's no doubt where he stands.
- It's astonishing that some today still pervert the gospel. Cults do this, for example. Yet they have this verse from Galatians in front of them!

---

12 Zodhiates, *The complete word study dictionary: New Testament.*

> Paul then returns to his credentials.

- Given their *heteros* gospel, who needs to be persuaded of the truth? Should Paul accept the gospel of the Galatians and go back to God to persuade Him to change *His* plans? Of course, it is a rhetorical question, as is the one that follows – Paul has never been a pleaser of men. He regularly says things that offend and does so unapologetically.

    o Paul makes the argument that if he were trying to persuade men, he would not be the *doulos*, the voluntary bondservant, of Christ. He would never have made that commitment. Yet, he has, and thus, is not trying to gain favor with men.

    - Paul liked to describe himself as a "bond-servant" (Greek *doulos*) in relation to Christ (Rom. 1:1; Phil. 1:1; Titus 1:1). This Greek word also describes Moses (Rev. 15:3), the Old Testament prophets (Rev. 10:7; 11:18), and the apostles (2 Cor. 4:5). Moreover, it describes Jesus Christ (Phil. 2:7), Christian leaders (1 Tim. 2:24), James (James 1:1), Peter (2 Pet. 1:1), and Jude (Jude 1). Furthermore, it describes John (Rev. 1:1), Christians (Acts 4:29; 1 Cor. 7:22; Gal. 4:7; Eph. 6:6; 1 Pet. 2:16; Rev. 1:1, 2:20), Tribulation saints (Rev. 7:3), and all believers (Rev. 19:2, 5; 22:3, 6) in the New Testament.[13]

    o He reminds us of Peter and John in Acts 4:13-22:

    13 Now when they saw the boldness of Peter and John, and perceived that they were unlearned and ignorant men, they marvelled; and they took knowledge of them, that they had been with Jesus. 14 And beholding the man which was healed standing with them, they could say nothing against it. 15 But when they had commanded them to go aside out of the council, they conferred among

---

13 Constable, T. (2003). *Tom Constable's Expository Notes on the Bible: Ga. 1:10*. Galaxie Software.

themselves, 16 Saying, What shall we do to these men? for that indeed a notable miracle hath been done by them is manifest to all them that dwell in Jerusalem; and we cannot deny it. 17 But that it spread no further among the people, let us straitly threaten them, that they speak henceforth to no man in this name. 18 And they called them, and commanded them not to speak at all nor teach in the name of Jesus. 19 But Peter and John answered and said unto them, Whether it be right in the sight of God to hearken unto you more than unto God, judge ye. 20 For we cannot but speak the things which we have seen and heard. 21 So when they had further threatened them, they let them go, finding nothing how they might punish them, because of the people: for all men glorified God for that which was done. 22 For the man was above forty years old, on whom this miracle of healing was shewed.

 Galatians 1: 11-17

11 But I certify you, brethren, that the gospel which was preached of me is not after man. 12 For I neither received it of man, neither was I taught it, but by the revelation of Jesus Christ. 13 For ye have heard of my conversation in time past in the Jews' religion, how that beyond measure I persecuted the church of God, and wasted it: 14 And profited in the Jews' religion above many my equals in mine own nation, being more exceedingly zealous of the traditions of my fathers. 15 But when it pleased God, who separated me from my mother's womb, and called me by his grace, 16 To reveal his Son in me, that I might preach him among the heathen; immediately I conferred not with flesh and blood: 17 Neither went I up to Jerusalem to them which were apostles before me; but I went into Arabia, and returned again unto Damascus.

➤ Having informed the Galatians that 1) they have turned away from Christ's grace, 2) they have turned away from the Gospel, and 3) that he is not going to try to please them by adjusting his gospel to theirs, Paul goes on to tell them his gospel isn't even his at all – it's the Lord's.

- **The important thing here is that Paul informs them that he didn't go to other men to seek his revelation (apokálupsis), just as he did at the opening of the letter. He received it directly from Christ.**

- Now we are going to get into a bit of Paul's bio. It's somewhat difficult to put together a definite timeline, but we will try.
  - Paul brings up what is clearly a difficult part of his past and something he regrets deeply – his persecution of the church. He held the coats while Stephen was stoned. We estimate this is sometime around AD 34.
  - On the road to Damascus, Paul received his vision (probably also around AD 34) and encountered Christ.
  - After he is healed, Acts tells us he began to *immediately* preach Christ in the synagogues. In other words, trying to reach his fellow Jews.
  - He makes the case that no one could have accused him of not being Jewish enough – he had studied under one of their greatest teachers, Gamaliel, and had excelled in honoring Jewish tradition.
  - Remember that Paul does try to preach to the Jews but is unsuccessful. And thus, God reveals to him that he is to have a ministry among the Gentiles. And how was he called? Through God's GRACE (there's that word again).

- Continuing on with his credentials, once he received the revelation of Christ, did he go check in with anyone in Jerusalem? No.
  - In fact, he goes to Arabia and it appears he spends time in the desert, studying and communing with the Lord, before returning to Damascus to preach once again.

Galatians 1: 18-24

> 18 Then after three years I went up to Jerusalem to see Peter, and abode with him fifteen days. 19 But other of the apostles saw I none, save James the Lord's brother. 20 Now the things which I write unto you, behold, before God, I lie not. 21 Afterwards I came into the regions of Syria and Cilicia; 22 And was unknown by face unto the churches of Judaea which were in Christ: 23 But they had heard only, That he which persecuted us in times past now preacheth the faith which once he destroyed. 24 And they glorified God in me.

- He's forced to flee in a basket (Acts 9:25) and then finally goes to Jerusalem. We think this is sometime around AD 37.

- He spends 15 days with Peter. The Greek word is only used once in the New Testament.

  - *historéō*; contracted *historṓ*, future. *historḗsō*, from *hístōr* (n.f.), knowing. To ascertain by inquiry and personal examination. This is the verb from which the English word "history" (*historía*) is derived. In the New Testament, to know or to visit, so as to consider and observe attentively and gain knowledge. Only in Galatians 1:18 ("to see," and hence become acquainted with). In Classical Greek, to narrate.[14]

  - It seems to indicate Paul was going there to get to know him. But NOT to have Peter explain the gospel. Can you imagine what their conversations would have been like?

  - It's interesting that Paul doesn't visit with any of the other apostles except James. But the reason he points this out must be that he's continuing to make the case that his gospel wasn't influenced by anyone else.

---

14 Zodhiates, *The complete word study dictionary: New Testament.*

- Paul spends his two weeks in Jerusalem, then leaves the region again. One can imagine why. Paul's reputation would still have been strong enough to evoke fear and doubt among the Jewish believers, who are the only ones in Judea.
  - Yet they heard about Paul. They heard how he had changed and was now preaching *for* what he had been *against*.
  - Are people aware of you with respect to the Gospel? Not, do they know you because you're a good singer or greeter or good at whatever your job is – do they know you by your fruit of bringing people to Christ?

CONCLUSION

- We take an awkward Chapter break in the middle of Paul's story, but it will continue in verse 1 of Chapter 2.
- But what have we learned so far? Chapter 1 contained a lot.
  - A terse greeting
  - An admonition that the Galatians have lost their way
  - A claim that his is the right gospel backed by a series of credentials including:
    - Direct revelation from Christ
    - No human influence
  - And running through the narrative, an emphasis on GRACE
- We sometimes take grace for granted. But I assure you Paul never did. Paul realized who he had been before Christ and who he was after his encounter on the way to Damascus. He never lost his gratitude and he never stopped preaching the true gospel. – WHAT ABOUT YOU?

GALATIANS CHAPTER 2

INTRODUCTION

> Last week, we started the book of Galatians. But before we dive in, let me ask you a question: How were you saved? Or perhaps more appropriately, by what were you saved?

- Ephesians 2:8-9 says, "For by grace are ye saved through faith; and that not of yourselves: *it is* the gift of God: Not of works, lest any man should boast."

- Is there anything else required? Absolutely not! Is there any alternative? No. That means that Buddhism, Hinduism, Islam – none of these are the same as Christianity and none offer another path to God. There's only one way and neither you, nor anyone else, can add anything to it. All other religions say, "You've got to *do* this or that to be right with God." Christianity says, "It's already done. Christ finished it. He paid the debt in full. All you have to do is accept what He's done and believe."

> That's perhaps *the* key point as we move into this letter!

- Recall that a group whom we call the Judaizers have asserted authority over the believers in the Galatian church. They are adding requirements that the believers must fulfill to be justified.

- Before grace, the Jewish connection with God was the Law.

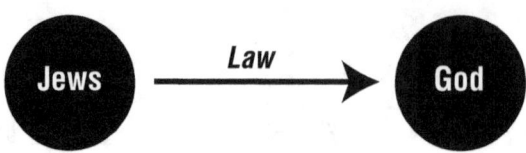

- Thus, it might be natural to assume that for Gentiles to be saved, they'd have to follow the Law as well.

- But Paul will make the case that Jews and Gentiles alike are saved by grace.

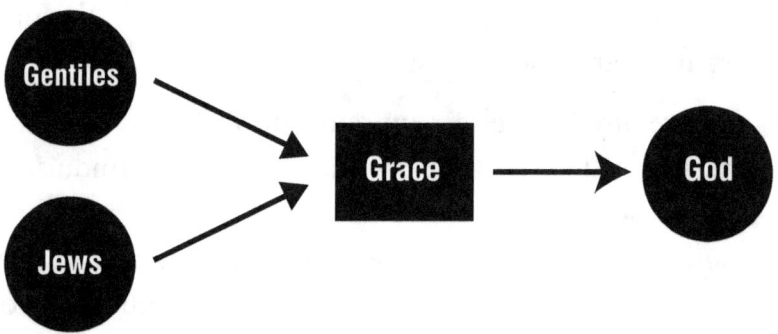

➤ To ensure that his argument will be accepted, Paul began introducing certain important credentials in Chapter 1:

- His claim as an Apostle
- His direct revelation of his gospel from Christ, not *any* man
- His lack of favoritism

➤ In Chapter 2, Paul will continue with providing credentials through additional biographical information and we are going to see a conflict that arose at one point with Peter in Jerusalem.

LESSON

 Galatians 2:1-5

> *2 Then fourteen years after I went up again to Jerusalem with Barnabas, and took Titus with me also. 2 And I went up by revelation, and communicated unto them that gospel which I preach among the Gentiles, but privately to them which were of reputation, lest by any means I should run, or had run, in vain. 3 But neither Titus, who was with me, being a Greek, was compelled to be circumcised: 4 And that because of false brethren unawares brought in, who came in privily to spy out our liberty which we have in Christ Jesus, that they might bring us into bondage: 5 To whom we gave place by subjection, no, not for an hour; that the truth of the gospel might continue with you.*

➤ "*Then*" – when?
- Recall that after Jesus confronted Paul on the road to Damascus, Paul spent time in Damascus, Arabia, Damascus a second time, and then went to Jerusalem for a brief period of two weeks.
- Then he's on the road again to Caesarea, then Tarsus, then Syria, then Cicilia.
- Around AD 47, he returns to Jerusalem very briefly to bring food to the church, which was extremely poor, and sets off on his two-year "First Missionary Journey" to Salamos, Pahphos, Antioch (Pisidia), Iconium, Lystra, Derbe.

- So it appears that around AD 50-51, Paul returns to Jerusalem again along with Titus and Barnabas. This is the visit he is talking about here. It is fourteen years after his first visit when he stayed for fifteen days.
- During this current visit is when we think it is possible the Jerusalem conference of Acts 15 occurs. However, it's unclear because when Peter visits Antioch later, his behavior is not consistent with the Acts 15 declarations.

➤ What caused him to go? *"Revelation"* – again the word *apokalupsis*, which Paul had already used in Chapter 1 to refer to the direct reception of his gospel from Jesus.
- Paul waits on Christ. How hard is that for us to do?! We always want to *do* something – travel, preach, launch another program, build a building. In fact, most of man's various religions are based on works.
- But Paul shows us that sometimes what we really need to do is have patience. Paul didn't go because he had been summoned by those in Jerusalem to explain his teaching. He went because Jesus told him to go.
- I don't believe we're waiting for a direct, personal revelation from Christ today. That time is past. But I do think God speaks to us through His word. And we certainly see plenty of examples of men of faith in the Scriptures who needed to exercise patience: Moses, Elijah, Daniel, etc. Patience truly is a virtue.

➤ When Paul arrives, it appears there are a number of conversations:
- There are many different groups involved in the conference according to this passage:
  - Paul's group – Paul, Barnabas, and Titus

- The leaders of the Jerusalem church which, from verse 9, would have included James, Peter, and John.
  - The group of *"false brethren"* – *pseudadelphos* – those who were causing trouble and who wanted, from verse 3, Titus to be circumcised as a Jew even though he was a Gentile.
- In the first conversation, there appears to be a public conversation where Paul "lays up" – communicates, makes known – the gospel that he had been preaching to the Gentiles (literally, the *ethnos* – the nations).
- However, there is also a *private* conversation with people Paul describes as those *"which were of reputation."*

➤ Paul's concern is that he had or might have *"run, in vain."* What does this mean?
- It seems unlikely that Paul's fear is that he was preaching a false gospel himself. He's already made the argument that his revelation came directly from Christ, so his gospel can't be *heteros* – a "different" (wrong) gospel.
- Paul also notes in 1 Corinthians 9:26 *"I therefore so run, not as uncertainly; so fight I, not as one that beateth the air:"* Paul knows what he's about.
- However, if the Judaizers had first agitated in Galatia and their philosophy was spreading to Jerusalem, Paul might be concerned that unless the Jerusalem leaders accepted his testimony, his mission would have been in vain. If the Jerusalem leadership had put the Gentiles under the Law, then the message of grace would have been lost.

➤ Paul tells us the false brothers had been brought in secretly – the word is used for smuggling- to the fellowship (at Galatia probably) to 'spy out' or thoroughly 'take aim at or mark' the behavior of the Believers in the fellowship.

- And their goal, to bring them into bondage-to thoroughly enslave.

- **καταδουλόω** *katadouloō*; contracted *katadouló*, future *katadoulṓsō*, from *katá* (2596), an intensive, and *douloō* (1402), to enslave. To enslave utterly, reduce to absolute slavery (2 Cor. 11:20); in the middle to make a slave for oneself (Gal. 2:4, *"that they might bring us into bondage"*)[15]

- How did Paul handle this? He persevered and overcame them. He didn't even submit to them for an hour and Titus didn't have to be circumcised.

✝ Galatians 2:6-10

> *6 But of these who seemed to be somewhat, (whatsoever they were, it maketh no matter to me: God accepteth no man's person:) for they who seemed to be somewhat in conference added nothing to me: 7 But contrariwise, when they saw that the gospel of the uncircumcision was committed unto me, as the gospel of the circumcision was unto Peter; 8 (For he that wrought effectually in Peter to the apostleship of the circumcision, the same was mighty in me toward the Gentiles:) 9 And when James, Cephas, and John, who seemed to be pillars, perceived the grace that was given unto me, they gave to me and Barnabas the right hands of fellowship; that we should go unto the heathen, and they unto the circumcision. 10 Only they would that we should remember the poor; the same which I also was forward to do.*

➤ After telling us how he withstood the false brethren, Paul goes on to tell us the rest of the outcome.

---

15 Zodhiates, *The complete word study dictionary: New Testament.*

- First, who are *"these who seemed to be somewhat"*? There are the people within the church at Jerusalem who were considered to be influential; they are the leaders in the church.
  - What does Paul tell us about them?
    - First, he doesn't really care whether they were influential or not. As we saw earlier in the letter, Paul is not a guy seeking to please men. He's not seeking favoritism or trying to "suck up" to the leaders. He doesn't seem to care.
    - Second, his basis for this is because *God* doesn't show favoritism. God doesn't esteem one man above another.
      - ✓ Paul here used an idiom that can be literally translated, "God does not accept the face of a man." To accept the face of someone is to evaluate that person on the basis of some outward appearance or external circumstance.[16]
      - ✓ On the one hand, in Galatians 1:17, Paul has already said there were apostles before him. So, Paul has already acknowledged their authority.
      - ✓ Yet, he's not going to just roll over and submit to that authority because he *knows*, not just thinks (he's had his revelation), that he's right.
      - ✓ Do we react the same as God to other people? Or do we look at outward appearances, titles, or wealth? Do we treat people better or differently when they have those things? Paul wouldn't have done that.

---

16 George, *Galatians*, 156.

> And after everything, these leaders "*added nothing*" to Paul's gospel. Nor did they take anything away. Rather, they extended the hand of friendship.
>   - First, they "*saw*" (having perceived by their senses) that Paul had been entrusted with the gospel.
>   - Furthermore, they agreed on the division of labor, recognizing Peter had been sent to the Jews (the circumcised) and Paul had been sent to the Gentiles (the uncircumcised). Note how Paul again works the idea of apostleship into the discussion. And keep track of that distinction between the circumcised and uncircumcised because it will be important throughout the book. The Judaizers were trying to convince the Gentiles that they needed to be circumcised to "get right" with God.
>   - We can see why Paul has the mission to the Gentiles. His previous behavior had compromised himself in front of other Jews. Either they would fear him or mock him for his conversion. And indeed, in Acts, Paul does preach in synagogues and is regularly run out of town.
>   - The only thing they ask is that Paul remember the poor which he had already been doing.

✝ Galatians 2:11-14

> *11 But when Peter was come to Antioch, I withstood him to the face, because he was to be blamed. 12 For before that certain came from James, he did eat with the Gentiles: but when they were come, he withdrew and separated himself, fearing them which were of the circumcision. 13 And the other Jews dissembled likewise with him; insomuch that Barnabas also was carried away with their dissimulation. 14 But when I saw that they walked not uprightly according to the truth of the gospel, I said unto Peter before them all, If thou, being a Jew, livest after the manner of Gentiles, and not as do the Jews, why compellest thou the Gentiles to live as do the Jews?*

> Having shown how he was accepted in Jerusalem, Paul has returned to Antioch. Then, Peter arrives for a visit.

> The Greek preposition beginning verse 11 suggests an opposition to what had gone before. In other words, whereas verses 6-10 indicated Paul and Peter were in agreement in Jerusalem, in Antioch, the situation was different. Or more accurately, became different.
> - From this incident, it's not clear whether the Acts 15 council has occurred yet. Recall that the decisions arising out of that (abstain from food sacrificed to idols, abstain from blood, and from sexual immorality) *should* have caused Peter to behave very differently.

> What was Peter's behavior when he arrived in Antioch?
> - He eats with the Gentiles and associates with them.
> - Despite being a Jew who had a very difficult time in Acts 10 understanding God's plan for Gentiles and how it would impact the Jews, Peter has been with the program and there appear to be no issues *until* other disciples arrive from Jerusalem.

- ➤ What happens when these other disciples arrive? Notice that Paul does not call them false brethren, but *"certain came from James."* So it suggests that they were officially sanctioned in their visit.
  - Upon their arrival, Peter separates himself and goes back to his old Jewish ways. Why? Because he's afraid of them. The Greek word *phobeo* should be a familiar word! We have many *phobias!*
  - It's pretty interesting, isn't it? These Jews have come from James in Jerusalem. Presumably, they have been instructed on what the protocol is around the Gentiles. Perhaps they simply didn't agree. And whoever they are, they are important enough that Peter is afraid of them. Maybe he is worried about what they will do to his reputation when he returns to Jerusalem. Even Barnabas falls into the trap.

- ➤ To Paul, this is a huge issue! One that is big enough to confront Peter as a leader publicly (no political correctness here!).
  - Peter's conduct is not 'in-step' with the gospel—literally, ὀρθοποδέω *orthopodéō;*
  - **ὀρθοποδέω** *orthopodéō:* contracted *orthopodṓ*, future. *orthopodḗsō*, from *orthópous* (n.f.), standing upright, which is from *orthós* (3717), right, level, and *poús* (4228), foot. To walk uprightly, correctly, carefully. Used figuratively in Galatians 2:14.[17]
  - Because Peter knows better, he is acting hypocritically. The word in verse 13 translated "hypocrisy" (*hypokrisis*) comes from the world of the theater, where it refers to the act of wearing a mask or playing a part in a drama. By negative transference it came to mean pretense, insincerity, acting in a fashion that belies one's true convictions.[18]

---

17 Zodhiates, *The complete word study dictionary: New Testament.*
18 George, *Galatians,* 177.

- ➤ Two issues are present here – one, the truth of the gospel, and two, the fellowship/unity of the church.
  - What is Paul's point? Before these men came, Peter was in fellowship with the Gentiles. He ate with them, fellowshipped with them, and did everything with them. The Law did not get in the way of any of his behavior (or that of Barnabas).
  - But with arrival of the Jerusalem brethren, he changed. And the question Paul asks is, "Peter, if you're going to 'switch teams,' do you want the Gentiles to switch too and become Jews?"
  - In fact, this isn't the first time Peter has turned around, is it? He did the same thing the night Jesus was taken. **It's a reminder that even those with authority can err.**
  - Why not confront Peter privately? Presumably, this is so that not only Peter is corrected, but also the men from Jerusalem. Additionally, the believers in Antioch benefit from the public rebuke as well. This restores unity within the body.

✝ Galatians 2:15-21

> 15 We who are Jews by nature, and not sinners of the Gentiles, 16 Knowing that a man is not justified by the works of the law, but by the faith of Jesus Christ, even we have believed in Jesus Christ, that we might be justified by the faith of Christ, and not by the works of the law: for by the works of the law shall no flesh be justified. 17 But if, while we seek to be justified by Christ, we ourselves also are found sinners, is therefore Christ the minister of sin? God forbid. 18 For if I build again the things which I destroyed, I make myself a transgressor. 19 For I through the law am dead to the law, that I might live unto God. 20 I am crucified with Christ: nevertheless I live; yet not I, but Christ liveth in me: and the life which I now live in the flesh I live by the faith of the Son of God, who loved me, and gave himself for me. 21 I do not frustrate the grace of God: for if righteousness come by the law, then Christ is dead in vain.

➤ Paul makes the point here that Peter ought to know better.

- First, he and Peter, as well as the other men from Jerusalem, are Jews, not *"sinners"* like the Gentiles. And what is the benefit of being a Jew? Having the Law, as well as the Prophets. They know who God is and have known since the beginning of their history. The Gentiles do not have any of that.

- But Paul would say, "We Jews know that no man can be saved by the Law!" Works do not deliver us. The Law only condemns the Jew.

- In fact, the Jews already knew this. Psalm 143:2 says, *"And enter not into judgement with thy servant: / For in thy sight shall no man living be justified."*

- What do we mean by Justification?

- ○ **Justification**: In its most basic meaning, "justification is the declaration that somebody is in the right."
- ○ "…Justification should not be confused with forgiveness, which is the fruit of justification, nor with atonement, which is the basis of justification. Rather it is the favorable verdict of God, the righteous Judge, that one who formerly stood condemned has now been granted a new status at the bar of divine justice."[19]
  - And so, we know that the Jew is justified through his faith in Jesus. But the Judaizers were asking these Gentiles to try and follow the Law, *knowing* it can't save them!
- ▸ Paul asks a rhetorical question: If I sin while I'm trying to be justified in Christ, does that make me an accessory? Of course not! His argument is as follows:
  - If the Law could have justified me, why did we need a Savior? Why not just rely on the Law?
  - Thus, if I return to the things I left (the Law) and try to rely on it for justification, then I make myself a sinner.
  - Furthermore, I impugn Christ along with me and make him a minister (Greek – *diakonos* – a deacon) of sin because I am appealing to my position in Christ while I commit this error.
    - ○ We see Paul's familiar response as he denies that Christ has anything to do with authoring sin.
    - ○ In fact, this is similar to what Paul says in Romans 6:1-4:

      6 What shall we say then? Shall we continue in sin, that grace may abound? 2 God forbid. How shall we, that are dead to sin, live any longer therein? 3 Know ye not, that so many of us as were baptized

---

19 George, *Galatians*, 191–192.

> *into Jesus Christ were baptized into his death? 4 Therefore we are buried with him by baptism into death: that like as Christ was raised up from the dead by the glory of the Father, even so we also should walk in newness of life.*

- Finally, Paul argues, "If I'm under the Law, then I can't get away from the Law unless I die." (Because who throws a dead body in jail for a speeding ticket?) But I died to the Law so I could live unto God. And I did that through Jesus' death on the cross. I died, but Christ is alive in me! And He did it because He loved me (Rom. 5-7)!

- What does it mean to have died to the Law?
  - First, Paul is speaking as a Jew to a Jew. He's not talking to the Gentiles or to you and me because we were *never* under the Law. But how many people do you know who think that they are going to a generic heaven stating reasons such as, "I'm a good person," "I try to live by the 10 commandments," or "I'm better than the next guy"? We Gentiles might not have the Law, but we do still fall back on moral codes and try to use them to justify ourselves.
  - Paul is now saying the Law no longer has rule over the Jewish believer in Christ. Before Christ, Paul was zealous for the Law. Now, he's learned that the Law isn't what has justified him, it's his faith in Christ.
  - He's not saying the Law has no value, and he will give us more perspective on that in coming chapters, but in the context of *justification,* the Law falls short.

- What is the effect of dying to the Law? Paul now lives to God through God's grace. As he says in Romans 6:14, *"For sin shall not have dominion over you: for ye are not under the law, but under grace."*

- Instead of living for the Law, always trying to be faithful to fulfill it (knowing one never could), the Jew is now free to truly live for God.

- And now we get to one of Paul's most important statements in Galatians 2:20, "*I am crucified with Christ: nevertheless I live; yet not I, but Christ liveth in me: and the life which I now live in the flesh I live by the faith of the Son of God, who loved me, and gave himself for me.*"

  - Paul is saying he was united with Christ in His death on the cross, dying to the Law and sin, and ultimately living to and for grace.

  - But if we died with Christ to sin and Christ lives in us, how is it that we still sin? Why doesn't Christ's presence in our lives keep us from sinning?

    - First, we still live in a fallen world and Christ's death did not change that. The reconciliation of creation to God's perfection hasn't occurred yet (though it will.) So, sin still exists and we, being of free will, can still choose to sin. And we do.

    - Our position in Christ is that we are *justified* through His death. This means we are saved from the penalty of sin.

      - However, theologians discuss *salvation* in terms of three tenses.

        - I *am* saved (justified – once and done – from the penalty of sin);

        - I *am being* saved (sanctified – an ongoing process – being delivered from the power of sin)

- - ◆ I *will be* saved (glorified – a future state – being delivered from the presence of sin)
  - ✓ Thus, even though Christ lives in us, we still feel the effects of sin in our lives
  - And why do we enjoy this position with God? Because Christ agreed to follow through with the Father's plan of redemption and go to the cross for us out of love.

- ➤ The only way we can be considered righteous is through God's grace. We cannot put that aside because if there was ANY OTHER WAY, CHRIST DIED IN VAIN (Matt. 26, Luke 22, 1 Cor. 15)!
  - Remember that in Matthew 26:39, Jesus asks for the cup to pass: *"And he went a little further, and fell on his face, and prayed, saying, O my Father, if it be possible, let this cup pass from me: nevertheless not as I will, but as thou wilt."*
  - Yet the cup did not pass. So, we are left with a number of possibilities. Either:
    - It was *not* possible—this was the only way
    - Or it was possible, but the Father did not answer the Son's prayer and let Jesus go through the cross even though He didn't have to. This second alternative is unfathomable.
  - The fullness of Scripture supports the first alternative; this was the only way. Christ did *not* die in vain – not for Paul, not for the Jews, and not for us.

- ➤ So, does Peter accept the rebuke? Evidently, he did. In fact, he will even write in his own letter in 2 Peter 3:15-16:

  > *15 And account that the longsuffering of our Lord is salvation; even as our beloved brother Paul also according to the wisdom given unto him*

hath written unto you; 16 As also in all his epistles, speaking in them of these things; in which are some things hard to be understood, which they that are unlearned and unstable wrest, as they do also the other scriptures, unto their own destruction.

- In this verse, we can see that Peter has clearly accepted Paul.
- Note also that he associates Paul's writing with Scriptures!

CONCLUSION

➤ We are not done with questions of works of the Law versus dependence upon grace. In the next Chapter, Paul will expound further.

➤ But what have we learned in Chapter 2?

- First, anyone can err – even someone in authority. Peter likely did not set out to introduce or create a problem on purpose, but he did.
- Second, when an error is introduced, it is important to correct it, even if it requires a public confrontation. Note that this was not simply a difference of opinion in how to interpret the Scriptures; it was a fundamental misunderstanding which, if allowed to continue, would have gutted the gospel.
- Third, Peter was mature enough to accept the correction. No matter how important you are, if you are wrong, accept a rebuke with grace, acknowledge it, and seek forgiveness (2 Tim. 3:16).
- Fourth, and most importantly, the Law cannot save you. Works cannot save you. Keeping the commandments cannot save you. The Five Pillars of Islam cannot save you. Oprah cannot save you. This is the theme of Galatians. Only Christ can save you – now and forever!

GALATIANS CHAPTER 3

INTRODUCTION

- Let's review where we were at the end of Chapter 2 (remembering that when Paul wrote his letter, there were no chapter divisions).
  - Paul has warned that the Galatians have departed from the gospel that he had preached to them. They had left it for "*another*" – a *heteros* gospel – another of a different kind.
  - Paul has made a strong case that the gospel he had preached is the true gospel. In fact, he provides his credentials as proof:
    - He is an apostle, meaning he had direct contact with Christ.
    - His title of "*apostle*" was not given to him by men.
    - The gospel that he preached was not given to him by men, nor did Paul initially even confer with the other apostles about it.
    - When he did finally go to Jerusalem, neither Peter nor James nor anyone of the other apostles in Jerusalem corrected what Paul was teaching. In fact, they not only extended the right hand of fellowship to Paul, but they recognized a division of labor in spreading the gospel: Peter to the Jews and Paul to the Gentiles.

- Nevertheless, not all was well:
  - As we have said, someone was teaching a different gospel. These were the *Judaizers* – Jews who had entered the fellowship and were preaching that Gentiles had to become Jews in order to be justified before God.
  - They were setting up a two-class system within the Church.
  - What's worse is that Peter, and even Barnabas who was Paul's traveling companion, had fallen under the spell at one point. These apostles, who certainly knew that God had a plan for the salvation of the Gentiles, had re-segregated themselves with their fellow Jews.
  - This caused Paul to confront Peter publicly in order to correct him, and Peter accepted that correction.
  - The point Paul makes at the end of the chapter, which he'll develop further in chapter 3, is that if salvation comes by works, like following the Law, then it renders grace irrelevant. And Paul is having none of that.

LESSON

 Galatians 3:1-9

> *3 O foolish Galatians, who hath bewitched you, that ye should not obey the truth, before whose eyes Jesus Christ hath been evidently set forth, crucified among you? 2 This only would I learn of you, Received ye the Spirit by the works of the law, or by the hearing of faith? 3 Are ye so foolish? having begun in the Spirit, are ye now made perfect by the flesh? 4 Have ye suffered so many things in vain? if it be yet in vain. 5 He therefore that ministereth to you the Spirit, and worketh miracles among you, doeth he it by the works of the law, or by the hearing of faith? 6 Even as Abraham believed God, and it was accounted to him for righteousness. 7 Know ye therefore that they which are of faith, the same are the children of Abraham. 8 And the scripture, foreseeing that God would justify the heathen through faith, preached before the gospel unto Abraham, saying, In thee shall all nations be blessed. 9 So then they which be of faith are blessed with faithful Abraham.*

> Paul is using a series of rhetorical questions as a literary device in his dialogue with the Galatians.

> How does Paul begin this section? *"O foolish Galatians, who has bewitched you?"*

- **Foolish:** ἀνόητος *anóētos*; genitive *anoḗtou*, masculine–feminine, neuter *anóēton*, adjective from the privative *a* (1), without, and *noéō* (3539), to comprehend. Lacking intelligence, foolish; one who does not govern his lusts, one without *noús* (3563), mind, the highest power of knowledge in man, the organ by which divine things are comprehended and known or ignored, being the ultimate seat of error (Luke 24:25; Rom. 1:14;

Gal. 3:1, 3; 1 Tim. 6:9; Titus 3:3; Septuagint: Deut. 32:31; Ps. 49:13; Prov. 15:21; 17:28).[20]

- In fact, the idea is that they are under a spell. They've been put under a spell by the evil eye, and have fallen away from the teaching that Christ was crucified for their sins.

> Paul takes them right back to the beginning of what he taught them – that Jesus Christ had been crucified. And he ties their original acceptance of the gospel of grace through Christ's death, burial, and resurrection to the gift of the Holy Spirit, which we saw throughout Acts.

- A key question here is: "How did you receive the Spirit?" Did you receive because you believed in the message you heard? Or did you receive it because of some work you did, some checklist under the Law that you completed?
    - Having begun their spiritual journey resting in the faith of this truth, they have reverted to trying to justify themselves before God based on how good they are at following rules.
    - The key here is that they had heard the message. They were not directly exposed to the resurrected Christ, but they believed His messenger.
    - Romans 10:14-17 says:

        14 How then shall they call on him in whom they have not believed? and how shall they believe in him of whom they have not heard? and how shall they hear without a preacher? 15 And how shall they preach, except they be sent? as it is written, How beautiful are the feet of them that preach the gospel of peace, and bring glad tidings of good things! 16 But they have not all obeyed the gospel. For Esaias saith, Lord, who hath believed our report? 17 So then faith cometh by hearing, and hearing by the word of God.

---

20 Zodhiates, *The complete word study dictionary: New Testament.*

- What have the Galatians begun? And what does it mean to be made perfect?
  - By accepting Christ, the Galatians had been justified, or declared righteous in God's sight. Nevertheless, they weren't sinless. None of us are. Sinlessness is not attainable, is it? We will be sinners all of our lives. But Scripture tells us in Philippians 1:6: *"Being confident of this very thing, that he which hath begun a good work in you will perform it until the day of Jesus Christ."*
    - WHO will complete that good work? Not us. Not by anything we do. But the Lord will. That is what we can be confident of even when we have our worst, most sinful day.
  - Paul is not speaking of physical or mental perfection. The word means 'completeness' and is used both here and in Philippians in terms of spiritual maturity.
  - Our journey does not *end* when we accept Christ and His cross, it *begins*. The Great Commission told Jesus' followers to go and make *disciples*. And a disciple is one who tries to emulate the teacher. Too many times, the Church falls short on that part of the Great Commission. We preach, we bring people to Christ, but after that, we tend to treat it like Mission Accomplished, when we still have an ongoing mission!
- Paul makes the point here that if they could have accomplished this by the flesh, by physical works or acts of obedience, then all of their suffering will have been in vain. What suffering?
  - Certainly, the believers (both Jews and Gentiles) had undergone persecution as a result of their conversions. The Jews were always causing problems when the gospel was preached.

- Yet Paul's use of the rhetorical questions indicates that they had *not* suffered in vain.
- His letter to the Ephesians states his case. Ephesians 1:13-14 reads:

  > *13 In whom ye also trusted, after that ye heard the word of truth, the gospel of your salvation: in whom also after that ye believed, ye were sealed with that holy Spirit of promise, 14 Which is the earnest of our inheritance until the redemption of the purchased possession, unto the praise of his glory.*

- Having believed, they were sealed immediately!

➤ Paul repeats his argument again – God has given you the Spirit through your acceptance of His Son through faith by hearing. Do not go back to the flesh! Do not return to works!

➤ Paul's use of Abraham represents a *personal* argument in the form of Abraham's example. Why appeal to Abraham? Because Paul is fighting the Judaizers and one key thing that Jews always fell back on was they were "sons of Abraham." We see this in John 8:37-41:

> *37 I know that ye are Abraham's seed; but ye seek to kill me, because my word hath no place in you. 38 I speak that which I have seen with my Father: and ye do that which ye have seen with your father. 39 They answered and said unto him, Abraham is our father. Jesus saith unto them, If ye were Abraham's children, ye would do the works of Abraham. 40 But now ye seek to kill me, a man that hath told you the truth, which I have heard of God: this did not Abraham. 41 Ye do the deeds of your father.*

- And of course, Jesus accuses them of being the sons of the devil.
- Like the Pharisees who confronted Jesus, the argument Paul is setting forth must have been surprising and difficult for the Judaizers to accept. Knowing that, Paul continues to make his

case and will use six Old Testament quotes in the next set of verses to show *from the Scriptures* that what he is saying about Law versus Grace is true.

- Genesis 15:6: *"And he believed in the Lord; and he counted it to him for righteousness."*
  - If the Judaizers want to appeal to Abraham, Paul takes them all the way to the beginning – when Abram was an unsaved Gentile whom God called.
- What did Abraham believe that justified him before God? In his very calling, in Genesis 12:1-3, God tells him:

  > *12 Now the Lord had said unto Abram, Get thee out of thy country, and from thy kindred, and from thy father's house, unto a land that I will shew thee: 2 And I will make of thee a great nation, and I will bless thee, and make thy name great; and thou shalt be a blessing: 3 And I will bless them that bless thee, and curse him that curseth thee: and in thee shall all families of the earth be blessed.*

  - Abram believes God in so much that:
    - He leaves his country and family.
    - He believes that God will make a great nation of him.
    - He believes that all nations will be blessed through him.
    - This is the good news that Abram received – not the Gospel we have today, but clearly a part of it – that all nations would be blessed through him because of the Messiah predicted in Genesis 3. That Messiah would come through Abraham's people.
  - Has he been circumcised? Not yet! Abraham will not get circumcised until Genesis 17 when he is ninety-nine years old.

So, Abraham wasn't justified because he'd been circumcised (as the Judaizers were suggesting).

- In fact, Abraham believes God so much that he agrees to sacrifice his own son in Genesis 22. He will offer Isaac up because God commands it. How can he do this? Because God had promised to make a great nation of Abraham in Chapter 12 and again in Chapter 17. Circumcision was a sign of that covenant but was not a condition of God offering it.

- Abraham's faith is detailed in Hebrews 11, the Hall of Faith.

> *8 By faith Abraham, when he was called to go out into a place which he should after receive for an inheritance, obeyed; and he went out, not knowing whither he went. 9 By faith he sojourned in the land of promise, as in a strange country, dwelling in tabernacles with Isaac and Jacob, the heirs with him of the same promise: 10 For he looked for a city which hath foundations, whose builder and maker is God. 11 Through faith also Sara herself received strength to conceive seed, and was delivered of a child when she was past age, because she judged him faithful who had promised. 12 Therefore sprang there even of one, and him as good as dead, so many as the stars of the sky in multitude, and as the sand which is by the sea shore innumerable.*

- Thus, Paul makes that argument that sons of Abraham are not sons because they are genetic descendants of Abraham; they are sons if they have faith like Abraham. For the Galatians and Gentiles today, that means hearing the message of the gospel and believing on it for justification.

- We can also look at Romans 4, where Paul uses a similar argument related to Abraham:

> *4 What shall we say then that Abraham our father, as pertaining to the flesh, hath found? 2 For if Abraham were justified by works,*

> *he hath whereof to glory; but not before God. 3 For what saith the scripture? Abraham believed God, and it was counted unto him for righteousness.*

- Again, Paul quotes Genesis 15:6 in Romans and makes the case that if Abraham had been declared righteous because of what he had done, then God would have "owed him." In other words, a workman is owed the fruits of his labor. If righteousness were based on works, God would owe us that reward in exchange for what we have done. But we are not justified because we do something (like circumcision), we are justified because of the grace God provides.

- From this, we understand that:
  - God foretold that all nations, including the Gentiles, would be saved as early as Genesis 12.
  - Although Abraham was obedient to his call to leave his country and to the command to be circumcised, his obedience was not what saved him.

- How then can the Judaizers appeal to this to try force the Galatian believers to put themselves under the Law to be saved?
  - Paul says they cannot do this. True sons of Abraham are those saved by faith, as the Galatian believers had been.

Galatians 3:10-14

> *10 For as many as are of the works of the law are under the curse: for it is written, Cursed is every one that continueth not in all things which are written in the book of the law to do them. 11 But that no man is justified by the law in the sight of God, it is evident: for, The just shall live by faith. 12 And the law is not of faith: but, The man that doeth them shall live in them. 13 Christ hath redeemed us from the curse of the law, being made a curse for us: for it is written, Cursed is every one that hangeth on a tree: 14 That the blessing of Abraham might come on the Gentiles through Jesus Christ; that we might receive the promise of the Spirit through faith.*

› In contrast to seeing that those who believed through faith were saved, we see Paul continue in verse 10 by telling us that those who have relied on the Law are the under the curse.

- He quotes Deuteronomy 27:26 by telling the Galatians that those who do not continue in ALL things of the law is cursed.
- This must also have been difficult for the faithful Jew to hear: "How can it be that I, who have strived to follow the Law my whole life, am actually under a curse?"
- Paul answers this by reminding the reader that unless one follows *everything* under the Law, he's not followed the Law at all.
- James tells us the same thing in James 2:10 which says, *"For whosoever shall keep the whole law, and yet offend in one point, he is guilty of all."*
- In fact, Paul tells us that even in the Old Testament it was known that the Law did not justify. We know this because he quotes Habakkuk 2:4 – *"the just shall live his by faith."*

- What, then, do we take away from this about those faithful Jews who believed under a pre-gospel dispensation?
- Jews were under the Law; there is no question about that. If you were not following the Law, you had no shot at all.
- But if you did, were you saved – at least in terms that we use? The Bible does not really speak about that. We know in Luke 16, that Lazarus is in Abraham's Bosom, while the rich man went to *"the torments of Hades"* and saw Abraham *"afar off."* We know that Christ tells the thief on the cross that he will be with him today in *"Paradise"* (Luke 23:43).
- This seems to suggest that when the Jew died, there were two options: a place of torment or Paradise. But is Paradise the same as heaven, and is the place of torment hell?
- Unfortunately, that's also hard to be definitive about because there are two other references to Paradise in the NT:
  - 2 Corinthians 12:2-4 states:

    2 I knew a man in Christ above fourteen years ago, (whether in the body, I cannot tell; or whether out of the body, I cannot tell: God knoweth;) such an one caught up to the third heaven. 3 And I knew such a man, (whether in the body, or out of the body, I cannot tell: God knoweth;) 4 How that he was caught up into paradise, and heard unspeakable words, which it is not lawful for a man to utter.

  - Revelation 2:7 says to the church at Ephesus: *"He that hath an ear, let him hear what the Spirit saith unto the churches; To him that overcometh will I give to eat of the tree of life, which is in the midst of the paradise of God."*

  - In the 2 Corinthians passage, Paul seems to equate Heaven and Paradise. In the Revelation passage, it also seems to suggest they are the same.

- There are two general views:
  - First is that Paradise and Heaven are different and that when Jesus died, he cleared out Paradise and took those faithful with Him to heaven. In this case, Heaven and Paradise could be different locations from Creation through Christ's death and then co-located following that. Faithful Jews went to Paradise when they died before the dispensation of Grace.
  - The second view is that Paradise and Heaven are the same and always have been.
- For our purposes, it does not really matter, other than that Paul is emphasizing his point that it is faith, not following the Law, that justifies.

- He continues this in Galatians 3:12, stating again that Law (works) and Faith are mutually exclusive.
  - Here, Paul quotes Leviticus 18:5: *"Ye shall therefore keep my statutes, and my judgments: which if a man do, he shall live in them: I am the Lord."*
  - Wiersbe says, "But someone might argue that it takes faith even to obey the Law; so Paul quotes Leviticus to prove that it is doing the Law, not believing it, that God requires (Lev. 18:5). Law says, 'Do and live!' but grace says, 'Believe and live!' Paul's own experience (Phil. 3:1–10), as well as the history of Israel (Rom. 10:1–10), proves that works righteousness can never save the sinner; only faith righteousness can do that."[21]

---

21 Wiersbe, W. W. (1996). *The Bible exposition commentary: Vol. 1* (pp. 699-700). Wheaton, IL: Victor Books.

- ▶ Paul has given them the bad news first: no one can be saved by the Law, being a son of Abraham in the tradition of the Law is no help, and if you want to try to save yourself by works, you're cursed.
  - ▪ But now the good news – Christ has already redeemed us from the curse by becoming the curse for us.
    - ○ The word for "redeemed" is *exorgazo*—to buy out of. Some of your translations may have "ransomed."
    - ○ Paul quotes from Deuteronomy 21:23 saying that everyone who hangs on a tree is cursed.
      - ◆ Not necessarily a cross or even a tree: **3586. ξύλον** *xúlon*; genitive *xúlou*, neuter noun from *xúō* (n.f.), to scrape. Wood, generally for fuel, timber (1 Cor. 3:12; Rev. 18:12; see Gen. 22:3, 6ff.). Anything made of wood: a staff, club (Matt. 26:47, 55; Mark 14:43, 48; Luke 22:52); stocks or wooden blocks with holes in which the feet and sometimes the hands and neck of prisoners were confined (Acts 16:24; Sept.: Job 33:11); a stake, cross, equivalent to *staurós* (4716), stake, post[22]
        - ✓ However, it is translated the same way in Acts 5:30 and 10:39.
        - ✓ See also 2 Corinthians 5:21: *"For he hath made him to be sin for us, who knew no sin; that we might be made the righteousness of God in him."*
        - ✓ And 1 Peter 2:24: *"Who his own self bare our sins in his own body on the tree, that we, being dead to sins, should live unto righteousness: by whose stripes ye were healed."*

---

22 Zodhiates, *The complete word study dictionary: New Testament.*

- And here's the key – two "So whats?"
  - First, so that the blessing of Abraham (the justification through belief/faith in the works of God, not man) can be conferred upon us.
  - And second, so that we also can receive the promise of the Spirit.
  - Note how Paul ties the mention of the Spirit in faith here to how he opened Galatians chapter 3 – how did the Galatians receive the Spirit? Through Faith, not works!

 Galatians 3:15-18

> *15 Brethren, I speak after the manner of men; Though it be but a man's covenant, yet if it be confirmed, no man disannulleth, or addeth thereto. 16 Now to Abraham and his seed were the promises made. He saith not, And to seeds, as of many; but as of one, And to thy seed, which is Christ. 17 And this I say, that the covenant, that was confirmed before of God in Christ, the law, which was four hundred and thirty years after, cannot disannul, that it should make the promise of none effect. 18 For if the inheritance be of the law, it is no more of promise: but God gave it to Abraham by promise.*

➤ Paul moves on now to give a human example – the idea of a contract. Because his readers might have said, "Okay, so Abraham was justified by faith. So what? The Law came later and it has to supersede Abraham's faith."

- He begins by reaffirming the relationship between himself and the Galatians; they are still brothers.
- Then he reminds them that if we draw up a contract and that contract becomes valid or established, you can't change that contract after the fact. We can argue about interpretation,

perhaps, and often do in court. But the basic nature of the contract remains the same.

- So, if the covenants of man cannot be changed, why would we ever think that covenants given by God to Abraham back in Genesis could be changed?
  - Yet most mainstream denominations do just that. They believe that God's promises to Israel have either been annulled or transferred to the Church. Neither is the case! Paul makes that point here by saying that not even the Law, which came 430 years after the promises of Genesis, could annul those promises!

- Who were the promises made to? Clearly Abraham, but who is the Seed?
  - The word is singular – *spermata*.
  - Perhaps Paul is wanting to counter the Jewish argument that Jews as a people would assume they were the subject of the promise.
  - But if we look to some context, we can see that Paul's conclusion – that the Seed is Christ – makes sense:
    - Genesis 22:18 – *"And in thy seed shall all the nations of the earth be blessed; because thou hast obeyed my voice."* SINGULAR NOUN: Seed
    - Genesis 12:7 – *"And the Lord appeared unto Abram, and said, Unto thy seed will I give this land: and there builded he an altar unto the Lord, who appeared unto him."* SINGULAR NOUN: Seed
    - Genesis 13:15 – *"And Lot also, which went with Abram, had flocks, and herds, and tents."* SINGULAR NOUN: Seed

- Genesis 24:7 – "*The Lord God of heaven, which took me from my father's house, and from the land of my kindred, and which spake unto me, and that sware unto me, saying, Unto thy seed will I give this land; he shall send his angel before thee, and thou shalt take a wife unto my son from thence.*" SINGULAR NOUN: Seed

- This reminds Paul's Jewish readers that justification would always come through Jesus – the promised Seed.

- G.R. Osborne writes:

> The emphasis in this verse is the seed of Abraham. The phrase "Abraham and his seed" stems from Genesis 13:15; 15:18; and 17:8, where the land promises are found. In Genesis the "seed" is a collective singular noun referring to Abraham's innumerable offspring, but Paul uses rabbinic logic to argue that "seed" is a singular noun. Such an argument was fairly common in Jewish exegesis. This prepares Paul's readers for 3:29 ("If you belong to Christ, then you are Abraham's seed"). It was common in Judaism to refer to the Messiah as "the seed of David" (2 Sam 7:12), so Paul is using common Jewish forms of exegesis to make his point that all of the Abrahamic promises are fulfilled in Christ.[23]

- Finally, Paul concludes with another logical argument. If we receive the inheritance (the Spirit and our position as justified) as a result of following the Law, then we are owed it. It is a result of our own obedience. There is no grace there. But God gave it to Abraham in advance! Abraham had not done anything to deserve the promise and could not do anything; he was going to get it as a result of God's faithfulness, not his own.

---

23 Osborne, G. R. (2017). *Galatians: Verse by Verse* (p. 99). Bellingham, WA: Lexham Press.

Galatians 3:19-25

> 19 Wherefore then serveth the law? It was added because of transgressions, till the seed should come to whom the promise was made; and it was ordained by angels in the hand of a mediator. 20 Now a mediator is not a mediator of one, but God is one. 21 Is the law then against the promises of God? God forbid: for if there had been a law given which could have given life, verily righteousness should have been by the law. 22 But the scripture hath concluded all under sin, that the promise by faith of Jesus Christ might be given to them that believe. 23 But before faith came, we were kept under the law, shut up unto the faith which should afterwards be revealed. 24 Wherefore the law was our schoolmaster to bring us unto Christ, that we might be justified by faith. 25 But after that faith is come, we are no longer under a schoolmaster.

- It makes perfect sense that after developing his argument that it is faith (through grace) that saves and not the Law, his readers might ask the question Paul raises in Galatians 3:19 – what good is the Law?
  - We've already seen that the Law:
    - Did not bring the Holy Spirit (Gal. 3:5)
    - Does not make anyone righteous before God (Gal. 3:11)
    - Is not a vehicle of faith, but of works (Gal. 3:12)
    - Does not provide the inheritance (Gal. 3:18)
  - Great, so why was it given in the first place? *"Because of transgressions."*
    - What does this mean? Paul is telling us that the Law was given to man in order that we might define and recognize sins.

- The IVP commentary has a good example:

  > Imagine a state in which there are many traffic accidents but no traffic laws. Although people are driving in dangerous, harmful ways, it is difficult to designate which acts are harmful until the legislature issues a book of traffic laws. Then it is possible for the police to cite drivers for transgressions of the traffic laws. The laws define harmful ways of driving as violations of standards set by the legislature. The function of traffic laws is to allow bad drivers to be identified and prosecuted.[24]

- In Romans, Paul tells a few more interesting things:
  - Romans 3:20 – *"Therefore by the deeds of the law there shall no flesh be justified in his sight: for by the law is the knowledge of sin."* (Note: no article – in Greek, this is any law, not the Law)
  - Romans 4:14-15 –

    > *Nevertheless death reigned from Adam to Moses, even over them that had not sinned after the similitude of Adam's transgression, who is the figure of him that was to come. But not as the offence, so also is the free gift. For if through the offence of one many be dead, much more the grace of God, and the gift by grace, which is by one man, Jesus Christ, hath abounded unto many.*

  - Romans 5:20 – *Moreover the law entered, that the offence might abound. But where sin abounded, grace did much more abound.*

- Paul tells Timothy something similar in 1 Timothy 1:8-11:

  > *8 But we know that the law is good, if a man use it lawfully; 9 Knowing this, that the law is not made for a righteous man, but for the lawless and disobedient, for the ungodly and for sinners,*

---

24 Hansen, G. W. (1994). *Galatians* (Ga 3:19). Downers Grove, IL: InterVarsity Press.

for unholy and profane, for murderers of fathers and murderers of mothers, for manslayers, 10 For whoremongers, for them that defile themselves with mankind, for menstealers, for liars, for perjured persons, and if there be any other thing that is contrary to sound doctrine; 11 According to the glorious gospel of the blessed God, which was committed to my trust.

- ♦ So, what is using it lawfully? It must be used to point out where someone is misaligned with God.

- Was the Law ever meant to be permanent? No. First, we know that it wasn't even put in place until 430 years after the promises to Abraham. Second, Paul tells us that the Law was only meant to be in place until the Seed (Messiah) should come.

- Interesting side point that Paul makes – the Law was appointed through angels. Did you know that? Don't we typically think of the God writing the Ten Commandments with His finger in front of Moses? And yet this was a tradition among the Jews and the same or similar statements either suggest or make explicitly clear their role in a number of places:

    - Deuteronomy 33:1-2 – *"And this is the blessing, wherewith Moses the man of God blessed the Chilfren of Israel before his death. And he said, The Lord came from Sinai, And rose up from seir unto them; He shined forth from mount Paran, And he came with ten thousands of saints:"*

    - Psalm 68:17 – *"The chariots of God are twenty thousand, even thousands of angels: The Lord is among them, as in Sinai, in the holy place."*

    - Acts 7:52-53 – *"Which of the prophets have not your fathers persecuted? And they have slain them which shewed before of the coming of the Just One; of whom ye have been now the betrayers and murderers; Who have received the law by the disposition of angels, and have not kept it."*

- Hebrews 2:2 – *"For if the word spoken by angels was stedfast, and every transgression and disobedience received a just recompence of reward;"*
- Paul is making the case that the Law is inferior because it came through the hands of mediators as opposed to grace, which comes directly from God.
  - God → Angels → LAW → Moses → the people (two mediators: angels and Moses)
  - God → Abraham (no mediator; God is the direct instrument)
  - Remember also that the blessings conferred by the Law were conditional-based on the faith of the people in upholding the Law. But God's promise to Abraham and to us is unconditional – only believe.
  - "Although countless explanations have been put forth for these two cryptic statements, Paul's meaning is essentially clear: the law is not on the same par with the covenant of promise not only because it was chronologically limited but also because it was handed down by angels with a man acting as a go-between."[25]
  - And yet Paul tells us we *do* have a mediator in 1 Timothy 2:5-6 – *"For there is one God, and one mediator between God and men, the man Christ Jesus; 6 Who gave himself a ransom for all, to be testified in due time."*
  - Of course, the key here is that God and Christ are one, so no third parties are needed. (Deut. 6:4 – *"Hear o Israel, the Lord our God is one."*)

---

25 George, *Galatians*, 256.

- So, if we have the Law on the one hand and the promises of God on the other, do they work in opposition to one another? Is the Law standing in opposition to the promises?
  - No, Paul says, "Certainly not." God is never inconsistent in His nature, unlike Allah who is described as capricious.
  - In fact, in regard to the Law, we are told, "Do this and live." The problem that Paul has already pointed out to us is that we *cannot* do it. We're simply not capable of it.
- Now Paul makes a transition to something positive because he argues that the Scriptures have taken "all things" and "shut them up" under sin. In other words, everything under the sun is in jail and sin is the jailor.
  - This idea that all are under the penalty of sin is found both in the Old Testament and the New Testament.
    - Psalm 143:2 – "*And enter not into judgement with thy servant: For in thy sight shall no man living be justified.*"
    - Romans 3:23 – "*For all have sinned, and come short of the glory of God;*"
    - Romans 5:12 – "*Wherefore, as by one man sin entered into the world, and death by sin; and so death passed upon all men, for that all have sinned.*"
  - And why? in order that the promise would be given to those who believe.
    - No discussion here of "the elect." Believe in the Lord Jesus, and you will be saved. Period. But you must give up your reliance on the Law.
- Paul goes on to finish up his description of how the Law has worked.

- Before faith came, the Law served as a guard.
  - For whom? Not for Gentiles. Remember – we were never under the Law. Thus the "*we*" here must be Paul's fellow Jews.
  - The Law had confined all (INCLUDING GENTILES) under sin and then served as the prison guard, keeping the faithful (JEW) safe until Christ arrived as the fulfilment of the promise.
  - Safe from what/who? Themselves.
- Not only as a guard, but as a tutor:
  - The word here is **παιδαγωγός** *paidagōgós*; genitive *paidagōgoú*, masculine noun from *país* (3816), a child, and *agōgós* (n.f.), a leader, which is from *ágō* (71), to lead. An instructor or teacher of children, a schoolmaster, a pedagogue (1 Cor. 4:15; Gal. 3:24, 25). Originally referred to the slave who conducted the boys from home to the school. Then it became a teacher or an educator. The ancient Greeks regarded a philosopher as a teacher, but not necessarily as *paidagōgós*.[26]
  - Hansen states, "In Paul's day the pedagogue was distinguished from the teacher *(didaskalos)*. The pedagogue supervised, controlled and disciplined the child; the teacher instructed and educated him."[27]
  - The idea is someone who has guardianship of a child until that child reaches adulthood. But it is not in terms of educating the child; rather the pedagogue delivered consistent discipline to regulate the way a young person behaved.

---

26 Zodhiates, *The complete word study dictionary: New Testament*.
27 Hansen, *Galatians*.

- o Hansen continues, "Josephus tells us of a pedagogue who was found beating the family cook when the child under his supervision overate. The pedagogue himself was corrected with the words: 'Man, we did not make you the cook's pedagogue, did we? but the child's. Correct him; help him!'"[28]
- o So, the Law's role was to deliver them to Christ, disciplined and spiritually mature. Its whole design was to be temporary, just like the pedagogue, to raise the child and then go away because faith = maturity.

➤ The Galatians had placed themselves back under the Law through the influence of the Judaizers. They had gone from being mature adults who had believed in Christ through faith to voluntarily taking on the role of wayward children who needed their pedagogue. They had eliminated the promise of Christ.

 Galatians 3:26-29

26 For ye are all the children of God by faith in Christ Jesus. 27 For as many of you as have been baptized into Christ have put on Christ. 28 There is neither Jew nor Greek, there is neither bond nor free, there is neither male nor female: for ye are all one in Christ Jesus. 29 And if ye be Christ's, then are ye Abraham's seed, and heirs according to the promise.

➤ Having made that point, Paul now encourages the Galatians by moving from "*we*" back to "*ye*" and by assuring them that they are now sons of God. They were no longer children and could enjoy all the privileges of adulthood if only they would grasp them.

➤ Paul now equates baptism with putting on Christ.

---

28 Ibid.

- And *if* we have put on Christ, *then* we can say there is no distinction between the Jew nor Greek, man nor woman, slave nor free. Thus, this applies to the church.
- In what way? Is he saying that men and women are the same or that Jews and Gentiles no longer have cultural differences? No. He is saying that they/we are all equal in terms of our justification before God.
- Remember how the Pharisees used to stand and pray, thanking God that they had not been made a woman or a Gentile? No more. God shows no partiality to those who are in Christ.
- This not only was good news for the Gentiles in Galatia, it meant that the Jews in Galatia also were free.
- However, **don't make this verse say more than it says in its context**. God still recognizes gender roles, roles within the church, roles within the family, the responsibilities of employers (slaveowners) and workers (slaves). It does not speak against slavery in the Empire, either.
- It also doesn't say anything about those who are outside of Christ. Specifically, it says nothing about Israel's position or future.

➤ Finally, Paul assures them that through their faith, they have become Abraham's seed, which, as we will recall, was based on faith and not biology.
  - There was no need for them to go through the Law to become Abraham's seed – through their faith, they had a direct line.
  - And thus, the Gentiles became heirs of all the benefits of being in Christ.

➤ Paul is going to continue developing this idea of sons and heirs in Chapter 4.

CONCLUSION

- Chapter 3 is complicated. To follow it, one really must understand Paul's internal dialogue as he asks himself a series of rhetorical questions based on answering the objections of the Judaizers. To fully appreciate his arguments, we also need to be versed well enough in Jewish arguments relating Abraham, faith, and justification. I have done my best to try to detail these, but Galatians is not a 101 course; it's more like a 301.

- But the main idea he has developed throughout the chapter is that it is grace that saves, not the Law. Yes, he defends the Law and argues that it was good and even necessary, but only until Messiah came.

- Chapter 4 will continue the doctrinal discussion before Chapters 5 and 6 become more practical. Hang in there!

GALATIANS CHAPTER 4

INTRODUCTION

➤ In Chapter 3, Paul began a complex argument about grace versus the Law. It is addressed primarily *to* the Jews in Galatia, but primarily *for* the benefit of the Gentiles.

➤ Beginning by asking who has "*bewitched*" these "*foolish Galatians*," he moves quickly to point out that the Law, which the Judaizers want to put the Galatian Gentiles back under, could not justify them, could not bring the Holy Spirit, and could not provide the inheritance that was promised. In the end, the Law was about works – works that no Jew could ever hope to fully perform. And recall that if one part of the Law was broken, then *all* of it was broken.

➤ At the end of the day, the works of the Law would amount to nothing. The promises God gave to Abraham, which predate the Law by 430 years, could not be cancelled or changed and would ultimately be fulfilled in the Messiah.

➤ What then, was the purpose of the Law? Paul tells us that it was a tutor, or more accurately a guardian, to keep "*us*" until the Messiah came.

- It's important to ask who the "*us*" is as the audience changes within the letter at various times. In general, the letter is addressed to the fellowship of believers in Galatia – both Jews and Gentiles.
- However, this doctrinal section, where Paul asks and answers rhetorical questions according to some internal dialogue, is primarily addressed to the Judaizers.
- He will switch back to addressing the congregation as we get further into chapter 4.

➤ In my view, this section of the letter is a strong argument *for* dispensationalism. Paul has told us that God has changed the way God is dealing with man. Before the Law were God's unconditional promises to Abraham. Four hundred and thirty years later, God gives Moses the Law (through angels, no less!). Now that Messiah has come, the Law is no longer of any effect. These are three different periods – three different manners in which God deals with man.

➤ Paul now continues his argument in Chapter 4, concluding the purpose of the Law. While he will once again discuss Abraham, he always brings it back to our true hope – Jesus Christ.

LESSON

 Galatians 4:1-7

> *4 Now I say, That the heir, as long as he is a child, differeth nothing from a servant, though he be lord of all; 2 But is under tutors and governors until the time appointed of the father. 3 Even so we, when we were children, were in bondage under the elements of the world: 4 But when the fulness of the time was come, God sent forth his Son, made of a woman, made under the law, 5 To redeem them that were under the law, that we might receive the adoption of sons. 6 And because ye are sons, God hath sent forth the Spirit of his Son into your hearts, crying, Abba, Father. 7 Wherefore thou art no more a servant, but a son; and if a son, then an heir of God through Christ.*

➤ I think that in these opening verses, Paul is still addressing all believers in Galatia. Why?

- Because he is continuing the argument that he began in the closing verses of Chapter 3 (remember – there are no chapter/verse divisions in the original letter – one could argue that a more natural break between Chapters 3 and 4 would be between verses 7 and 8 of Chapter 4).

- Galatians 4:1 references the heir that Paul concluded chapter 3 with in verse 29.

➤ Paul has already described how the Law was a guardian for the Jews and concluded Chapter 3 by saying that if you were baptized into Christ (through faith – always through faith – baptism alone does not save in this age of Grace), you are part of God's family. And if part of God's family, then you are an heir. Of what? Of the promises to Abraham.

- In other words, they are justified through faith the same way Abraham was justified through faith as discussed earlier in Chapter 3.
  - We do *not* take this to mean that the promises that God made to the Jewish people somehow devolve onto the church. That is not in evidence here or anywhere in the New Testament.

➤ So, you're an heir – great. But can you exercise the authority that goes with that heirship? Not if you are a child. In the Greek, this is a *nḗpios*; feminine *nēpía*, neuter *nḗpion*, adjective from *nḗ–*, not, and *épos* (2031), word. One who cannot speak, hence, an infant, child, baby without any definite limitation of age.[29]

- We can easily relate to the idea of someone being made an heir but not being of legal age to have access to the wealth or property he/she will eventually control.
- In fact, as someone under age in Roman society, the *nepios* is no better than a slave (a *doulos*). He has no rights and is not viewed as being responsible enough to control the inheritance.
- Yet he is still the master. Think of a child-king who has a regent that rules for him. You would still address the child as "Your Majesty," but the regent would actually make the decisions *until* the child comes of age.

➤ Paul has already likened the Law to the *paidagogos* – the disciplinarian whose job it was to keep the child on the straight and narrow.

- Now Paul gives us a picture of two other types of authority in the child's life:
  - ἐπίτροπος *epítropos*; genitive *epitrópou*, masculine noun from *epitrépō* (2010), to permit. Steward, manager, agent.

---

29 Zodhiates, *The complete word study dictionary: New Testament.*

A person entrusted to act in another's name or to whose care anything is committed by another (Matt. 20:8); a steward or treasurer to a prince, or a deputy governor, or a Roman procurator; a guardian to whom the care of orphans is committed, the same as *paidagōgós* (3807), a guardian (Gal. 4:2). In Luke 8:3, a manager of private affairs.[30]

- ♦ Note that though the definition says the same as a *paidagogos*, the role actually seems different in terms of responsibility.
- ♦ This is someone who guides/guards the child and is responsible for the protection of the child.

○ And the **οἰκονόμος** *oikonómos*; genitive *oikonómou*, masculine noun from *oíkos* (3624), house, and *némō* (n.f., see *aponémō* [632]), to deal out, distribute, apportion. An administrator, a person who manages the domestic affairs of a family, business, or minor, a treasurer, a chamberlain of a city, a house manager, overseer, steward.[31]

- ♦ We get 'economy' from this word.
- ♦ This role as separate from the *epitropos* suggests a more economic function in terms of protecting the estate.

■ Paul's readers might have different views about when the son might become a legal adult and pass from under the care of the stewards.

○ In Judaism, when the boy turned thirteen, he went through a ceremony known as the *bar miṣwāh*, literally meaning "son of the commandment." We know it under the name that came about in the 19th century – the *bar mitzvah*. Girls go

---

30 Ibid.
31 Ibid.

through the *bat mitzvah* at the age of twelve. In both cases, it was a ceremony that signaled the child was an adult and responsible to follow the Law. Note that an actual ceremony is not necessary – the right of passage is automatically triggered by age.

- o In Greek society, the age was later, often seventeen or eighteen. This is the age at which a young man could enter the military.
- o In Roman society, the age was variable. This may be why Paul speaks of *"the time appointed of the father."*
  - ◆ If this is so, it leads one to think that Paul is referring primarily to the Roman custom as he observed that a child is under guardians and trustees until the time set by his father. A Roman child became an adult at the sacred family festival known as the Liberalia, held annually on the seventeenth of March. At this time, the child was formally adopted by the father as his acknowledged son and heir and received the *toga virilis* in place of the *toga praetexta* which he had previously worn. [32]
  - ◆ The Greek term is **προθεσμία** *prothesmía*; genitive *prothesmías*, feminine noun from *pró* (4253), before, and *thesmós* (n.f.), custom, which is from *títhēmi* (5087), to set, place, lay. **A pre–appointed day or time,** *the day or time being understood* (Gal. 4:2).[33]

➤ Galatians 4:3 – the use of *"we"*

- Does Paul mean, "we Jews"? Possibly – he had been talking to the Judaizers back in Chapter 3.

---

32 Boice, *Galatians*, 471.
33 Zodhiates, *The complete word study dictionary: New Testament.*; emphasis added

- Or does he mean "we" the inclusive of both Jews and Gentiles?
  - I think we might tend to make this selection as Paul had switched to being more inclusive at the end of Chapter 3. In Galatians 3:26, he says: *"For ye are all the children of God by faith,"* there being neither Jew nor Greek.
- In either case, the *"we"* in question were *"in bondage under the elements of the world"*
  - "Elemental" [*stoicheia*] originally meant "to stand side by side in a row." It had a wide range of meanings in the Greco-Roman world of Paul's day: (1) the ABC's of a child's training or the elemental teachings of any subject (cf. Heb. 5:12; 6:1); (2) the basic components of the physical universe – air, water, fire, earth (cf. 2 Pet. 3:10, 12), which were often deified by the Greeks; (3) the heavenly bodies (cf. I Enoch 52:8–9); and this is how the early church fathers interpreted its use in Colossians 2:8, 20.[34] It could also have meant pagan deities.
  - "World" is the Greek *kosmos* – or universe.
  - It seems that if Paul had wanted to specifically talk to the Jews here, he would have referred back to the Law. Instead, he uses a broader analogy.
    - For the Jew, it could refer to the Law.
    - For the Greek, it could refer to pagan religion or basic philosophical principles.
    - Either way, both the Greek and the Jew were 'under age' when it came to the grace of the Father.

---

34 Utley, R. J. (1997). *Paul's First Letters: Galatians and I & II Thessalonians Vol. 11* (p. 43). Marshall, TX: Bible Lessons International.

- Paul now gives an encapsulated version of the gospel.
  - Christ came at the exact right time. In fact, Paul refers to it here as the *"fullness of time."* What characterized that?
    - A "worldwide" system of Roman roads to allow communication
    - The safety and security provided to travelers by the Roman army
    - A common language – *koine* Greek
    - Expansion of synagogues throughout the Mediterranean whereby the Jews demonstrated monotheism and an expectation of the Messiah
    - The passage of Daniel's 69 weeks
    - God is working in His time, just as He had done when He sent the Law 430 years after the promises to Abraham. Just as He did by allowing time to elapse between the promise of the Messiah in Genesis 3 and Abraham. We are on *His* timetable in all things.
  - Paul notes that *"God sent forth His son."* This tells us of Christ's divine nature.
  - At the same time, he notes Jesus' humanity by reminding his readers that Jesus was *"made of a woman."*
  - Born under law – never forgetting Jesus was a Jew (no "the" in the Greek)
  - He came for a specific purpose – to redeem those who were under law (no "the" in the Greek).
    - *"to redeem"* – Paul has used this before – to set free by paying a price

- ○ *"them that were under the law"* – presumably the Jews

  - ◆ Hence Paul's whole argument to the Galatian Gentiles – if Jesus came to redeem the Jews from under the Mosaic Law, why ever would you want to put yourself under the Law?

- ○ *"That we might receive the adoption of sons"*

  - ◆ I believe "*we*" here refers to both the Jews and Gentiles

  - ◆ Adoption of sons: **υιοθεσία** *huiothesía*; genitive *huiothesías*, feminine noun from *huiós* (5207), son, and *títhēmi* (5087), to place. Adoption, receiving into the relationship of a child. In the New Testament, figuratively meaning adoption, sonship, spoken of the state of those whom God through Christ adopts as His sons and thus makes heirs of His covenanted salvation. See *huiós* (5207)[35]

  - ◆ R.E. Picirilli, in his commentary on the book, writes:

    > We have to obtain a clearer understanding of this often misunderstood phrase, "adoption of sons." First, remove entirely from your mind the connotation of "adoption" in our modern world. We use the word to refer to the legal act which causes one to be a child of others not truly his parents. But that has absolutely nothing to do with what Paul means here.
    >
    > The whole phrase "adoption of sons" is a translation for a single Greek word which literally means *the positioning of a son*. This act was not applied in the Greek world to one who was *not* one's child by birth. It was an action applied to one's *own* child. It referred to that "time appointed" (verse 2) when the child matured and was released from the nursemaids. Now the child stood in a new position in his family as a mature son, no longer a small child.

---

[35] Zodhiates, *The complete word study dictionary: New Testament.*

Evidently such a practice was often followed in the world of Paul's day, especially in the wealthier households, and perhaps even by the Jews. We do know that the Jews still make a big occasion out of the time when a boy becomes "of age"; the special ceremony is now called *bar mitzvah* ("son of the law"). Even in the modern United States in high society, children are sometimes given such special occasions as "coming out" parties to "introduce" them to the adult world about them.

To such an idea Paul refers, and his point is that the advent of Christ introduced a new relationship between God and His family. **Whereas before God dealt with us as small children, under a nursemaid, now we have received the "son-placing" and are dealt with as mature sons in God's household. All the responsibilities and rights of adult sons are now ours.**[36]

- R.J. Utley, however, disagrees, applying this view to the Roman world:

    Paul used the familial metaphor "adoption" of our salvation while John and Peter used the familial metaphor "born again." The adoption metaphor was used primarily in two contexts in Roman culture. In Roman law, adoption was very difficult. A long, involved and expensive legal procedure, once enacted adoption afforded several special rights and privileges: (1) all debts were cancelled; (2) all criminal charges were dropped; (3) they could not be legally put to death by their new father; and (4) they could not be disinherited by their new father. In legal terms, they were a completely new person. Paul was alluding to the believers' security in Christ by using this Roman legal procedure (cf. Rom. 8:15, 23). When a father publicly adopted a son, he officially and permanently became his heir. Also, the metaphor was used in the official ceremony of a boy becoming a man, held on the 17th of March each year.[37]

---

36 Picirilli, R. E. (1973). *The Book of Galatians* (pp. 65-66). Nashville, TN: Randall House Publications.; emphasis added

37 Utley, *Paul's First Letters: Galatians and I & II Thessalonians*, 45-46.

- o However, Utley's last sentence does seem to agree with Picirilli's position.
- In either case, it is clear that Christ's foreordained arrival and sacrifice made it possible for both the Jew and Greek to now positionally become "sons of God" with all the privileges and responsibilities thereto.
- No longer under guardian, a tutor, or a steward!

➤ As a result of becoming a son, what do you get? You *are* still under something.
- The Holy Spirit – see Romans 8:14-17
- God sends the Spirit to our hearts and we are never without Him
- Note the Trinity here – God sends the Spirit of His Son. All three persons are found in one verse.
- This enables us to have a very special relationship with God, crying out "Father" as Jesus did in the garden.

➤ Therefore (Finally, we get to the end of this argument that started in Gal. 3:6.) – you are not a slave any more – neither as a Jew to the Law nor as a Gentile to either the Judaizers or pagan practices. You are an heir of God.
- D.K. Campbell makes an interesting point: "The plural forms in verse 6 were replaced by the singular forms in verse 7 thus making the application to the reader direct and personal. In God's family, sonship carries with it heirship (cf. Rom. 8:17)."[38]
- T. George also states:

---

38 Campbell, D. K. (1985). *Galatians*. In J. F. Walvoord & R. B. Zuck (Eds.), *The Bible Knowledge Commentary: An Exposition of the Scriptures: Vol. 2* (p. 602). Wheaton, IL: Victor Books.

"Therefore," because all of this is true, you are *no longer* a slave, but a son. You are no longer under subjection to the elemental spirits. No longer a minor heir with no rights to the inheritance. No longer is your relationship to God determined by your race, rank, or role. No longer are you under the harsh tutelage of the *paidagōgos*. No longer are you shut up in the prison house of sin. No longer are you under the curse of the law. The promise given to Abraham and fulfilled in his prophetic Seed, Jesus Christ, has now been extended to all of those who through faith in him have become sons, crying "*Abba!*" and heirs of the living God.[39]

 Galatians 4:8-20

8 Howbeit then, when ye knew not God, ye did service unto them which by nature are no gods. 9 But now, after that ye have known God, or rather are known of God, how turn ye again to the weak and beggarly elements, whereunto ye desire again to be in bondage? 10 Ye observe days, and months, and times, and years. 11 I am afraid of you, lest I have bestowed upon you labour in vain.

12 Brethren, I beseech you, be as I am; for I am as ye are: ye have not injured me at all. 13 Ye know how through infirmity of the flesh I preached the gospel unto you at the first. 14 And my temptation which was in my flesh ye despised not, nor rejected; but received me as an angel of God, even as Christ Jesus. 15 Where is then the blessedness ye spake of? for I bear you record, that, if it had been possible, ye would have plucked out your own eyes, and have given them to me. 16 Am I therefore become your enemy, because I tell you the truth? 17 They zealously affect you, but not well; yea, they would exclude you, that ye might affect them. 18 But it is good to be zealously affected always in a good thing, and not only when I am present with you. 19 My little children, of whom I travail in birth again until Christ be formed in you, 20 I desire to be present with you now, and to change my voice; for I stand in doubt of you.

---

39 George, *Galatians*, 309.

- Paul again talks about the previous nature of the Galatians. It is not clear to me whether he is back to referring to only the Gentiles or to the Jewish members of the congregation as well.
  - "*when ye knew not God*" – The word for "*knew*" is *eido* and means "to see with perception." The idea is that in the past, the Galatians did not *know* God as the one, true monotheistic Lord. They had not been exposed to Him in a way that they could understand who He was (or even *that* He was).
  - Instead, they served – literally, were under bondage (a word related to *doulos*, bondservant) – to things which were not by their nature gods.
    - It is interesting that Paul does not deny the existence of these things. What are they?
      - Can't we all say that we were under bondage to something before Christ? In this case, Paul is probably referring to the pagan deities which makes his lack of denial of their existence all the more interesting. These would be demonic forces.
      - But for us, and most today, we have been under bondage to wealth, to politics, to career, to family, to exercise, to New Ageism – you name it.
      - No matter what it was, it was a form of bondage. Of covetousness. Of worship.
  - Paul contrasts this with their condition now:
    - They now know God, but a different word is used. Instead of *eidos* – seeing with perception – the word is *ginosko* – to know in a beginning or completed sense. The Galatians are beginning to understand who God is now.

- Paul also reverses the knowledge – they are under the blessing of God's grace and He now "*ginoskos*" them.
  - Did God not know them before? Of course He did. But now, as Paul has described in Galatians 4:7, the Galatians are not in servitude, but are sons and heirs; God knows them differently. The Galatians are now justified.
- And if they are justified, why would they turn back into slavery?
  - Once again, Paul uses the word *stoichion* in describing the powerless elements, the same as used in verse 3.
- He points out that they are doing this with purpose; they haven't just fallen into it.

➤ Then there is this odd verse about observing the days, months, season, or years. While not entirely clear, it is likely that Paul is referencing their renewed observance of the Jewish calendar and its holidays and festivals. This would fit in the overall context with Paul addressing the influence of the Judaizers.

➤ Paul is *phoboumai* from *phobos* meaning afraid, but also terrified. He is terrified that he labored (and somehow wore himself out) in vain (without purpose).

➤ Paul now switches to what several commentaries call a "personal appeal" to the Galatians.
- "*be as I am*;" An imperative, a command. How is Paul that they should become like him?
  - Freed from the Law through grace – He is a man who participated in murder and persecution who has found grace and has put aside works.

- Note that Paul does *not* say, "Become like *Jesus.*" The Galatian believers are to imitate Paul. This is reminiscent of Paul's admonition to the Corinthians in 1 Corinthians 11: 1 which says, "*Be ye followers of me, even as I also am of Christ.*" See also 1 Thessalonians 1:6 and Philippians 3:17.
  - Why would Paul urge them to imitate him and not Christ? Because they have no *personal* experience with Jesus. Recall that Paul, in the opening chapter of this letter, described his credentials as an apostle, which meant someone who had been in close physical contact with Jesus and had learned from Him directly. Paul fits the bill.
  - This makes the whole "What Would Jesus Do?" movement or line of thinking/acting particularly problematic for believers today. Jesus taught as one under the Law – a perfect fulfillment of it. Yet in His interpretation of that very Law, He acted on divine insight. Thus, when we get to John 8 and the episode with the adulterous woman, there is no contradiction between Jesus' compassion for the woman and his failure to uphold the Law by causing her to be stoned. He recognized the set-up by the Pharisees. One wonders how the outcome might have differed if the Pharisees had presented a legitimate case of true Law-breaking.
    - Nevertheless, to say today, "Well, Jesus would have done such and such" or "Jesus would *never* do X", frankly, displays a bit of arrogance in the speaker, or at best naiveté. To say, "If Jesus were at the border today, He would want us to take care of the children" is perhaps true, but at no time in Scripture do we find Jesus urging that Jews or Gentiles disobey

Roman or Jewish laws, whether they be religious, civil, or ceremonial. Jesus does not, for example, urge His followers not to pay taxes. Nor does He urge slaves to run away or incite rebellion against Rome for political reasons, which is something the Jews had come to expect of their Messiah.

- ✓ So, when someone today says, "Jesus would want *this* or *that*," or "I just follow Jesus," it's best to pause and really assess what that person is saying to see whether they have a clue. They likely don't. They are even more likely taking something Jesus said completely out of context. They mean well (and in today's society, isn't that just *everything*?), but are not rightly dividing the Word of God and are ascribing their motivations to God.

- ✓ What we *can* say, I think, that Jesus would want is for us to 1) believe in Him and call upon His name for salvation, 2) take the Bible seriously – study and exegete (not isogete), 3) spread the gospel, 4) love one another, and 5) submit to the authorities that are over us.

- "for I am as ye are"

    - This leads into the next set of verses and serves as a transition. Paul had become like them when he came to Galatia and ministered to them. He did not set himself apart, as Peter and Barnabas had and to whom he gave an admonishment. Rather, Paul was part of their very community.

    - Paul entered their community and spent time with them. But it is *incorrect* to say that Paul did not evangelize. We often hear the saying, "Preach the gospel, use words if necessary."

I think Paul would scoff at that. Words are *always* necessary to communicate the power of the gospel and convert hearers to Christ. Romans 10:14-15 says:

> *14 How then shall they call on him in whom they have not believed? and how shall they believe in him of whom they have not heard? and how shall they hear without a preacher? 15 And how shall they preach, except they be sent? as it is written, How beautiful are the feet of them that preach the gospel of peace, and bring glad tidings of good things!*

- They only way to become a believer is to hear the gospel proclaimed. We cannot simply be good examples and good neighbors and show people how much we care. Those things should flow out of our own commitment to Christ [created in Christ for good works (Eph 2:10)] but are not in and of themselves sufficient.

> In the context of becoming like them, Paul says that when he was with them, they did him no wrong. They did not offend him or act unjustly towards him.
- Indeed, Paul says he was physically ill when he came and preached to them. Young's Literal Translation has 'through'. Zodhaites defines this use of the Greek as somewhat unusual: (C) Of the manner or state, meaning through or during which anything takes place (Gal. 4:13, "through infirmity," i.e., during bodily weakness). This sense of diá is rare with the accusative and comes from the general idea of duration.[40]
  - So, in reading, it's not clear whether he came to them as a direct result of his illness or that when he fell ill, it was for some duration and he remained in Galatia evangelizing.

---

40 Zodhiates, *The complete word study dictionary: New Testament.*

- What was his illness? We know that in 2 Corinthians 12:7-9, Paul speaks about his *"thorn in the flesh"*:

  > 7 And lest I should be exalted above measure through the abundance of the revelations, there was given to me a thorn in the flesh, the messenger of Satan to buffet me, lest I should be exalted above measure. 8 For this thing I besought the Lord thrice, that it might depart from me. 9 And he said unto me, My grace is sufficient for thee: for my strength is made perfect in weakness. Most gladly therefore will I rather glory in my infirmities, that the power of Christ may rest upon me.

- But no further details are provided there and it's not clear that this illness is the same as what Paul speaks of in 2 Corinthians.

- There are three theories of what Paul's illness might be:

  - *Malaria.* This theory was advanced by W. Ramsay, who surmised that Paul may have contracted malaria when he first came into the swampy region of Pamphylia in southern Asia Minor. This was the occasion when John Mark became disillusioned with missionary life and returned home to Paul's great consternation (Acts 13:13). It may have been that Paul's original plan was to travel westward toward Ephesus and Greece but that he was redirected because of his illness toward the higher terrain around Pisidian Antioch. There, high above sea level, he found a more congenial place to recuperate. On this theory, Paul may still have been in the grips of a terrible fever when he first began his preaching mission in Galatia.

  - *Epilepsy.* The verb in Galatians 4:14 translated *"ye despised not"* literally means, "you did not spit out" (*ekptuō*). A common belief was that the evil demon that caused epilepsy could be exorcised or at least contained by spitting at the one thus possessed. On this reading, Paul was commending the Galatians for receiving him with courtesy and favor even though they may have witnessed the unpleasant sight of his epileptic seizures.

- ◆ *Ophthalmia.* In Galatians 4:15, Paul praised the Galatians for their willingness to tear out their own eyes and give them to him. This, together with Paul's reference in Galatians 6:11 concerning writing such large letters in his own hand, have led many scholars to believe that Paul's illness was some kind of serious eye disorder. But as F. F. Bruce has noted, "there can be no certain diagnosis" of Paul's ailment here, nor of his "*thorn in the flesh*", assuming the two are not to be identified.[41]
  - ○ While interesting to speculate, it's probably not particularly fruitful for us. The important things are that 1) Paul was ill, 2) the Galatians received him and treated him well, 3) Paul evangelized and they came to believe.
- Note in Galatians 4:14, some translations say Paul was received as an "*angel.*" Remember that in the Greek, "angel" is *angelos* and simply means "messenger," which would also fit. I don't think Paul was saying they received him as though he had been a supernatural being.
- Paul was their friend when he was there. They were saved through his preaching. They were joyous as a result. Now he was correcting them to get THEM back on the right path. Certainly, he wasn't doing that because he was their enemy and is reminding them of that.
  - ○ Paul is speaking "*truth,*" from the Greek *aletheuo*, meaning real, actual, not counterfeit.[42] He's giving them the real deal.

---

41 George, *Galatians*, 322-323.
42 Zodhiates, *The complete word study dictionary: New Testament*.

- Contrasting with what was real or genuine is what "*They*" were giving – a lie.
  - The "*they*," of course, are the Judaizers. They are certainly seeking after the Galatians zealously. Paul says the purpose is nefarious – to exclude or separate them from Paul and have them latch onto the Judaizers.
  - Paul says it's ok to be zealous, but for a good thing. And that they should continue in their desire for that good thing even though he had departed.
- Again, switching back to his own feelings for them, he calls them his "*little children*" – a term of endearment towards little children or a teacher to students.
  - He is laboring, as in giving birth, *again*. Interestingly, he appears to be expressing concerns once again that his earlier efforts may have been ineffective. Or perhaps he's saying he will continue to experience these labor pains until Christ has formed in them.
  - The word is **μορφόω** *morphóō*; contracted *morphṓ*, future. *morphṓsō*. from *morphḗ* (3444), form, shape. To form, fashion, originally used of artists who shaped their material into an image. Found only in Galatians 4:19 where the Christian is described as a little child who needs to mature until the very image of Christ be impressed upon his heart.[43]
  - Clearly, the Galatians hadn't reached that point.
- Finally, Paul wishes he was there with them at this crucial time. He would "*change his voice*" or tone to be able to reach them more effectively.
  - Why does he want to be there? He is, literally, perplexed

---

43 Ibid.

about them. The word *aporeo* implies having doubts, but also carries with it an idea of "not knowing how to proceed, determine, speak or act (John 13:22; Acts 25:20; 2 Cor. 4:8; Gal. 4:20; Septuagint: Gen. 32:8; Jer. 8:18)."[44]

- One can see why. Paul is far away, and the Judaizers are close by. What more can he do from where he is?
- Is he puzzled about the state of their salvation? Or about what further arguments he can use to convince them about the failure of law versus the benefit of grace?

 Galatians 4:21-31

> *21 Tell me, ye that desire to be under the law, do ye not hear the law? 22 For it is written, that Abraham had two sons, the one by a bondmaid, the other by a freewoman. 23 But he who was of the bondwoman was born after the flesh; but he of the freewoman was by promise. 24 Which things are an allegory: for these are the two covenants; the one from the mount Sinai, which gendereth to bondage, which is Agar. 25 For this Agar is mount Sinai in Arabia, and answereth to Jerusalem which now is, and is in bondage with her children. 26 But Jerusalem which is above is free, which is the mother of us all. 27 For it is written, Rejoice, thou barren that bearest not; break forth and cry, thou that travailest not: for the desolate hath many more children than she which hath an husband. 28 Now we, brethren, as Isaac was, are the children of promise. 29 But as then he that was born after the flesh persecuted him that was born after the Spirit, even so it is now. 30 Nevertheless what saith the scripture? Cast out the bondwoman and her son: for the son of the bondwoman shall not be heir with the son of the freewoman. 31 So then, brethren, we are not children of the bondwoman, but of the free.*

➤ Paul has given them his personal appeal – I came to you; I became as one of you; I taught you grace, and I still zealously desire that you

---

44 Ibid.

would continue in grace, leaving the bondage of the Law behind and putting the Judaizers aside.

> He now makes one last argument before moving into chapters 5 and 6 which deal with the more practical aspects of Paul's letter.

> In this argument, he turns once again back to the question he had asked in Galatians 4:9: *"But now, after that ye have known God, or rather are known of God, how turn ye again to the weak and beggarly elements, whereunto ye desire again to be in bondage?"*

> He also turns back once more to reference Abraham and builds an allegorical case between Law and Grace based on Ishmael and Isaac, the two sons of Abraham.

- First, Paul asks them *one more time*:
  - *"Ye that desire to be under* the *law"* – Note, again there is no article in the Greek. He appears to be accusing them that they simply want to be under some form of religious regulation. The Judaizers would put them under "The Law," but one wonders if they might have adopted any requirements put upon them by someone persuasive enough.
    - Note that by saying they still *"desire"* or have a mind to be under law; it indicates that they are not there yet – there is time to step back from the brink.
  - *"Do ye not hear the law?"* This time, the article *is* present.
    - To hear is *akouso* (like "acoustic") and means to hear, but in this case, to hear with comprehension. Paul is saying, "Don't you understand what the Law is going to do to you?"
  - Remember – Paul has said the Law is good, but inferior to what we have under Grace.

- Paul now introduces the story of Abraham and his two sons. In total, Abraham had eight sons. One from Hagar (Ishmael), one from Sarah (Isaac), and six from Keturah (Gen. 25:1-2) who was the woman he married after Sarah died. However, Paul is really only concerned with the Ishmael and Isaac – these are the keys to the biblical allegory and are of course key to how history has played out between the Arabs and the Jews.
  - Note that in Galatians 4:24, Paul tells us that these two births are symbolic or ἀλληγορέω *allēgoréō*; contracted *allēgorṓ*, future *allēgorḗsō*, from *állos* (243), another, and *agoreúō* (n.f.), to speak in a place of assembly, which is from *agorá* (58), market place. To allegorize, to speak allegorically where the thing spoken of is emblematic or representative (Gal. 4:24, "which things are said allegorically" [a.t.], or in a mystical sense).[45]
    - We didn't know it at the time, did we? We thought Ishmael was simply a picture of man trying to accomplish God's will in man's own way, under man's own plans and that Isaac was the miraculous child promised to Abraham and Sarah directly by God Himself.
  - Recall that Ishmael was born first (though Isaac would always be called the "firstborn"). He is born of Hagar and both he and Hagar are ultimately chased out of Abraham's camp because he "scoffs" at Isaac. Interestingly, one Jewish commentator suggests that the word in Hebrew has sexual overtones and that there may have been some kind of abuse going on. Nevertheless, Hagar and Ishmael are cared for by God and Ishmael fathers twelve sons who become the forbears of the twelve Arabic tribes (Gen. 25:13).

---

45 Ibid.

- Paul is making the case here that Ishmael is a slave because his mother is a slave (the son inheriting the character of the mother) and that Isaac is free (born of a free Sarah). Thus, despite the Law coming to the Jewish people through Moses, a descendant of *Isaac*, Paul is redefining the allegory or type to say that the those under law are in slavery like Ishmael was and those under grace are free like Isaac was.

- Let's make a table to compare the two covenants:

THE COVENANT OF THE LAW	THE COVENANT OF GRACE
Ishmael – born of man's effort akin to works under the Law	Isaac – born of God's direct promise to Abraham. A child of miracle since Sarah was barren.
Ishmael – born of slave, born into bondage like the Jews	Isaac – born free like those under grace
Hagar – corresponding to Mt. Sinai in Arabia where the Law was given, but also a symbol of Jerusalem in Paul's day, i.e., mother to and full of Jews still observing the Law and thus in bondage to it	Sarah – the "Jerusalem above"; mother to all those living under God's promise of grace
Represents the old covenant	Represents a new covenant[46]

---

46 I do not think this is the New Covenant spoken of in Jeremiah 31. *That* covenant is specifically with the House of Israel. *This* covenant is with the NT grace-filled Believer. Specifically, let's look at Jeremaiah 31:31-34:

> 31 Behold, the days come, saith the Lord,
> That I will make a new covenant
> With the house of Israel, and with the house of Judah:
>
> 32 Not according to the covenant that I made with their fathers
> In the day *that* I took them by the hand
> To bring them out of the land of Egypt;
> Which my covenant they brake,
> Although I was an husband unto them, saith the Lord:
>
> 33 But this *shall be* the covenant that I will make with the house of Israel;

- It's also worth a reminder that Isaac is a type of Christ:
    - Born of a promise from God to a mother who didn't expect it
    - Named before he was born
    - Persecuted by those "born of flesh" (Ishmael)
    - Given as an offering
    - Returned after the offering three days later (note that Isaac is not even in the narrative again until it is time for his bride)
- This is a bit of a reverse, isn't it, at least for the Jews. The Jews would have proudly seen themselves as sons of Abraham and Isaac – and would have thus thought they were in the right. But Paul has turned them on their ears and claimed them to be sons of Ishmael – in bondage still to the very Law of which they are so proud.
- The quote from Isaiah 54:1 –
    - The quotation from Isaiah 54:1 prophesied the changing fortunes of Israel, which Paul applied to Sarah's history.

> After those days, saith the Lord,
> I will put my law in their inward parts,
> And write it in their hearts;
> And will be their God,
> And they shall be my people.
>
> 34 And they shall teach no more every man his neighbour, and every man his brother, saying,
> Know the Lord:
> For they shall all know me,
> From the least of them unto the greatest of them, saith the Lord:
> For I will forgive their iniquity,
> And I will remember their sin no more.

Who is this covenant with? It says very specifically in v31—the House of Israel and the House of Judah—in other words, Jews. It's not the church. Why? Because the church doesn't exist yet. Is it in effect yet? No, we can look at the Jews today and clearly see that this prophecy is yet to be fulfilled. This is a post-rapture covenant that the Lord will make with faithful Jews. Jeremiah nor his readers would not have understood that this could apply to anyone but the Jewish people. LMA

Israel before her Babylonian Captivity was likened to a woman with **a husband**. The **barren woman** was Israel in Captivity. The woman bearing **more ... children** may have pictured Israel restored to the land after the Exile, but more particularly it portrays her millennial blessings. Paul applied this passage (he did not claim it was fulfilled) in this context to Sarah, who though previously barren, was later blessed with a child, and who would ultimately enjoy a greater progeny than Hagar.[47]

- In Galatians 4:28, Paul reminds the Galatian believers that they are child of the promise. He has already told them that those of faith are the true children of Abraham (and thus sons of God), but he is making one final push in his argument.

- Just as Ishmael persecuted Isaac, so the Judaizers are persecuting the Galatian believers by trying to put them back under the Law.

- What did Sarah do when this happened to Isaac? She told Abraham to get rid of Hagar and Ishmael. "*Cast out the bondwoman.*" And Abraham did. Paul is urging the Galatians to cast out the Judaizers once and for all and be heirs with the freewoman.

- In doing so, they will truly be free.

CONCLUSION

> Whew! We've made it through Chapter 4. We have only a few more verses in Chapter 5 dealing with this issue as Paul sums up everything and specifically will teach about circumcision, a practice the Judaizers wanted to instill in the Galatian community.

---

47 Campbell, *Galatians*, 604

➤ In Chapter 4, we have seen Paul continue his argument that we are sons of God and not slaves because we grow to maturity through Grace and not by Law; we have heard Paul's personal appeal that they abandon the Judaizers; and we have seen one final 'type' reminding Paul's readers that to fall back under Law was to discard the Promise of the age of Grace given by God.

➤ In Chapter 5, Paul will turn to talking about their liberty and love in Christ and will urge them to walk in the Spirit.

GALATIANS CHAPTER 5

INTRODUCTION

> In Chapter 4, Paul continued his arguments to the Galatians that they should be freed from the Law and reliant upon grace.

- He concluded his reasoning with respect to sonship and heirship of the Christian believer who had come to Christ through grace with an elegant summary of the entire gospel message in Galatians 4:4-5 and encouraged the Galatians that they were now sons and heirs who could call God "Abba, Father."

- Yet he continued to express his concerns for them – they had adopted "*days, and months, and times, and years*," an apparent reference to the Jewish calendar and its holidays.

- And of course, there remains the issue of circumcision, which Paul will address in Chapter 5.

- Paul worried that he had preached grace in vain as the Judaizers who were "*zealously affect[ing]*" them and seemed to be have a greater influence.

- He also explained two covenants to them and surprisingly (at least from a Jewish standpoint) argued that the Judaizers were really under the bondsman's covenant (Ishmael) while Christians in Grace were under the freeman's covenant (Isaac). This is the complete opposite of what a righteous Jew would have believed.

- Thus, Paul urged them to *"be as I am,"* not like the Judaizers. Live in the grace and freedom afforded them through Christ. This is a key message for Christians today and one often ignored as we wrestle with questions about how Jesus would respond to this or that social crisis. Christians understandably want to follow Jesus, to be "little Christs," yet the Scriptures don't always provide us the detailed insight we need to do this. We are limited by our 21st century Gentile, American viewpoint as we look at a first century Jewish rabbi who was both man and God. If we "rightly divide" the Word, we realize that much of what Jesus taught in the Gospels was specifically to Israel and for her benefit rather than the church. Hence Paul's admonition here and elsewhere (c.f., 1 Cor. 11) to follow or become like him as he follows Christ, providing us a true example of Christian living.

- Chapter 5 will transition into instructions regarding Christian living and includes the famous verses about the characteristics of the "fruit of the Spirit."

  - But we aren't *quite* done with Paul's arguments about Law and Grace. The first part of the chapter will bring the issue to conclusion.

  - The latter part of the chapter discusses how we are to behave in the Spirit.

LESSON

 Galatians 5:1-6

> *5 Stand fast therefore in the liberty wherewith Christ hath made us free, and be not entangled again with the yoke of bondage. 2 Behold, I Paul say unto you, that if ye be circumcised, Christ shall profit you nothing. 3 For I testify again to every man that is circumcised, that he is a debtor to do the whole law. 4 Christ is become of no effect unto you, whosoever of you are justified by the law; ye are fallen from grace. 5 For we through the Spirit wait for the hope of righteousness by faith. 6 For in Jesus Christ neither circumcision availeth any thing, nor uncircumcision; but faith which worketh by love.*

➤ Galatians 5:1 could be said to be the summary for the entire second section of Paul's letter.

- Recall that the first segment (Chapters 1 and 2) were autobiographical and laid out Paul's history and qualifications to teach.
- This second section is about Law versus grace.
- The final section (most of Chapter 5 and then Chapter 6) are instructions on how to live.
- Galatians 5:1 contains two commands:
    - *"Stand fast therefore"*
        - Because we are children of the freewoman (the end of Chapter 4), we are to enjoy the liberty that comes through Christ.
        - This is an 2nd person, present tense, imperative command, meaning:

- ✓ It applies to all of Paul's readers (i.e., "you" or "all y'all")
- ✓ It is not a suggestion or request
- ✓ It is an action which is meant to be done on a continuous basis as opposed to a "once and done" type of action
    - In what are we to *"stand fast"*? The liberty by which Christ has made us free.
    - The word for liberty is *eleutheria* – a word for freedom and used in this context as being released from the religious requirements of the Law. It shows up a second time in this verse as a verb where Christ has made us free.
  - *"be not entangled"*
    - The same verb form – 2nd person plural, imperative, present tense
    - The verb means to be held, but in this case, *"entangled"* is a good translation
    - Entangled in or by what? The *'yoke of bondage'* or even slavery.
- If, in fact, Christ has set us free, we are to enjoy that liberty.
  - Recall that in John 8:36, Jesus had already told the Jewish leadership that *"If the Son therefore shall make you free, ye shall be free indeed."* The context was not dissimilar to Paul's arguments here. Jesus had been confronted by the Jews about who He was and what He was teaching. The Jews relied on their lineage as Abraham's sons for their authority – Jesus' authority came from above. Ultimately, the Jews

then never accepted Jesus' Messiahship and crucified Him. In Galatia, the Judaizers hadn't accepted grace.

- Note the slightly different construction of the ESV and other modern translations. Here we see a separation between the purpose of what Christ has done (i.e., He has set us free in order that we might enjoy that freedom) and the commands that follow from the purpose. I think the message is the same – don't give up your liberty/freedom to put yourself back under a set of rules that don't do anything for you. That applies equally to rules under the Jewish Law as it does to rules, guidelines, and rituals imposed by a particular denomination.

> Paul seems to make a jump to the subject of circumcision in Galatians 5:2, a subject he has not addressed since back in Chapter 2.

- He says, "*Behold*," from the verb for "to behold." The NIV's "Mark my words" is not a literal translation, but an interpretation. However, Paul does seem to be saying here something to the equivalent of: "Heads up, guys; this is important!"

- He then stresses (or re-stresses) his own authority on the subject. "*I, Paul*" am delivering this message. It's important and I have the authority, so pay attention.

- And that message is that circumcision is of no benefit to the believer.

    o But wait, didn't Paul have Timothy circumcised back in Acts 16:3? Why did that happen?

        ◆ First, we remember that Timothy is half Jewish (mother) but also half Greek (father). So, he was not circumcised at birth because the Greeks didn't do that – circumcision set you apart as Jew. Timothy would have been viewed as a Greek by other Jews.

- However, in Acts, we are transitioning from a focus on Jews (present through the Gospels) to the new "church" as it comes into being. Where does Paul go when he arrives in town? To the synagogue. To his Jewish brethren. He has not yet switched his focus to gentile believers. And if he brings with him the half-Jewish Timothy, will he get very far in his preaching? No. So, Timothy is circumcised *not* because it is salvific in any way, but because to fail to do so would have had negative repercussions on their ministry. **There is no contradiction between what Paul is saying to the Galatians and his actions in the Book of Acts.**
- So what Paul is telling them is that if they think that getting circumcised somehow gives them "salvation points" or puts them in a better stead, they're wrong.
  - If you put yourself back under the Law by requiring circumcision, you've missed the entire point of grace.
- Paul again makes this clear by reminding them that if they want to follow this little piece of the Law *and rely on it for salvation*, they've got to follow the whole Law completely or it's of no effect. And of course, no one can follow the whole Law. Remember back in Galatians 3:10 that Paul had quoted an Old Testament text reminding the reader that "*Cursed is everyone that continueth not in all things which are written in the book of the law to do them.*"

- "*Christ is become of no effect unto you*"
  - The verb here is *katargeo* and means to render useless, ineffective. One way to think about what Paul is saying is to say, "You can't have half-Christ and half-Law. If you want circumcision and the Law, it is that or nothing. But if you

want Christ and grace, that is *also* all or nothing. There's no middle ground." Consider:

No middle ground or overlap!

- *"fallen from grace."*
    - This phrase causes some debate. Does this mean that they had lost their salvation? Or is there something else going on?
    - The verb is *ekpipto* and in the figurative sense, means to fall from any state or condition, i.e., to lose one's part or interest in that state; followed by the genitive [Gal. 5:4; 2 Pet. 3:17; Rev. 2:5 (Textus Receptus)][48]
    - It makes sense in Paul's context – the Galatian believers would have lost their interest in grace by following the Law. They would exchange one for the other.
    - Randy White makes a note on this verse: "Compare 'fallen' (*ekpipto*) from other synonyms Paul could have used to see that he does not mean 'you have lost your salvation' but 'you have left the teaching of Grace and gone to the teaching of the law.'"[49]
        - ✓ Other words Paul might have used to convey the idea of loss of salvation are: *athetéō* (114),

---

48 Zodhiates, *The complete word study dictionary: New Testament.*
49 R. White, Exegetical Notes. Galatians 5:4. Logos Bible Software. Accessed July 28, 2019.

to reject, set aside; *akuróō* (208), to render void, cancel; *exoudenóō* (1847), to set at naught; *kathairéō* (2507), destroy, pull down; *katargéō* (2673), to render useless or inactive; *kenóō* (2758), to make empty; *husteréō* (5302), to come behind in or be inferior.[50]

✓ All except the latter might be much stronger and convey a different idea.

♦ It's worth noting that you might find some theologians who would argue that Paul *is* saying that the Galatians have lost their salvation (but could get it back again by abandoning the Law in favor of grace). This is a difficult position to hold, in my view, because one would spend one's life never being certain of anything, potentially bouncing back and forth between saved and unsaved.

➤ Paul concludes this little section by reminding the Galatians that it is through/by the Holy Spirit that we await the *"hope of righteousness"* which is the Resurrection. And we do this by faith, not Law.

- In contrast with legalists, true believers **by faith** (not works) **eagerly await** (*apekdechometha;* used seven times in the NT of the return of Christ: Rom. 8:19, 23, 25; 1 Cor. 1:7; Gal. 5:5; Phil. 3:20; Heb. 9:28) the consummation of their salvation (cf. Rom. 8:18–25).[51]

- It doesn't matter whether you're circumcised or not (remember, Paul has already told us there is no Jew or Gentile *in Christ*). It just matters if you have the faith to believe.

- "Avails nothing" means "has no power."

---

50 Zodhiates, *The complete word study dictionary: New Testament.*
51 Campbell, *Galatians*, 605

- "*Love*" here is *agape*.
- Again, Paul is not saying here that works save, but that works flow out of faith through love "working" – *energeo* – producing an effect or being operative.
  - Remember Paul in Ephesians 2:8-10: "*For by grace are ye saved through faith; and not of yourselves: it is the gift of God: not of works, lest any man should boast. For we are His workmanship, created in Christ Jesus unto good works, which God hath before ordained that we should walk in them.*"
    - We're created for these good works!
  - And James, who told us in Chapter 2:17-18: "*Even so faith, if it hath not works, is dead, being alone. Yea, a man may say, Thou hast faith, and I have works: shew me thy faith without thy works, and I will shew thee my faith by my works.*"

 Galatians 5:7-15

7 Ye did run well; who did hinder you that ye should not obey the truth? 8 This persuasion cometh not of him that calleth you. 9 A little leaven leaveneth the whole lump. 10 I have confidence in you through the Lord, that ye will be none otherwise minded: but he that troubleth you shall bear his judgment, whosoever he be. 11 And I, brethren, if I yet preach circumcision, why do I yet suffer persecution? then is the offence of the cross ceased. 12 I would they were even cut off which trouble you.

13 For, brethren, ye have been called unto liberty; only use not liberty for an occasion to the flesh, but by love serve one another. 14 For all the law is fulfilled in one word, even in this; Thou shalt love thy neighbour as thyself. 15 But if ye bite and devour one another, take heed that ye be not consumed one of another.

> Paul takes a softer tone here as he commends the Galatian believers.
  - The verb for *"run"* is in the imperfect tense. The website "Precept Austin" describes the imperfect tense this way:
    - "The **Imperfect tense** denotes continuous, ongoing or repeated action in past. Thus the imperfect tense often «paints» a vivid picture of an action («motion picture») as one which happens over and over."[52]
    - And provides some examples:

      > Mark 4:37 And there arose a fierce gale of wind, and the waves **were breaking over** (imperfect tense) the boat so much that the boat was already filling up.
      >
      > **Comment**: Can't you picture yourself in the boat with the waves pounding again and again (imperfect tense conveys this picture) against the side and even beginning to fill the boat with water.
      >
      > Luke 9:16 Then He took (aorist) the five loaves and the two fish, and looking up (aorist) to heaven, He blessed (aorist) them, and broke (aorist) them, and **kept giving (imperfect)** them to the disciples to set before (aorist) the people.
      >
      > **Comment**: The blessing and breaking of the loaves and fish happened in a moment of time, while the "giving" of the bread and fish occurred over and over, which paints a vivid picture of the miraculous nature of the event. Try to place yourselves in the disciples' "sandals" for a moment![53]

  - In this case, we might translate Galatians 5:7 by saying "You were running well over time and you had kept running." But then…
  - But as he did earlier in Chapter 3, Paul asks who has hindered

---

52 Precept Austin. (2018, Aug. 4). Greek Quick Reference Guide. Retrieved from http://www.preceptaustin.org/greek_quick_reference_guide

53 Ibid.

them. He lays the blame at the feet of the Judaizers because the hindrance could certainly not have come from the one who called them – Jesus.

- Then he quotes a proverb which we understand clearly: "*A little leaven leaveneth the whole lump.*" Paul also uses this in 1 Corinthians 5:6.
  - Leaven is yeast. To introduce just a small amount of it into the dough causes the whole loaf to rise. Levitically, it was a type for sin because it corrupted by puffing up. Recall that at the Passover, all leaven was removed from the home (Ex. 12:15). Jesus warned against the "leaven of the Pharisees and Sadducees" (Matt. 16:11).
  - It seems clear that Paul is implying that the teaching about circumcision is the "*little leaven*" that threatens to corrupt the entire Galatian church.

➤ Back in Galatians 4:20, Paul said he had had his doubts about the Galatians. But now, in Chapter 5, Paul is convinced of them that they will pursue the right path.
  - This leads me to lean on the interpretation of Galatians 4:20 as Paul is unsure of how to proceed with them in terms of being able to convince them.
  - It appears that Paul's confidence comes from the Lord.

➤ But Paul issues a warning to those who are troubling the church – literally "stirring things up" as in a pool – that person (or persons) will bear the judgement of trying to lead them astray. This is a warning reminiscent of Jesus warning that those who led the children astray would be better off with a millstone hung around their necks and dropped into the ocean (Matt. 18:6).

- Do you know people like this in the church today? Sure you do. Always trying to stir up a bit of trouble through gossip, through meddling, through playing "devil's advocate." How do we handle them?
- Many times, it's best not even to engage with them:
    - Proverbs 14:7 – *"Go from the presence of a foolish man, / When thou perceivest not in him the lips of knowledge."*
    - Proverbs 9:6 – *"Forsake the foolish, and live; / And go in the way of understanding."*
    - Proverbs 26:4 – *"Answer not a fool according to his folly, / Lest thou also be like unto him."*
- Yet sometimes, Scripture does tell us how to deal with these folks.
    - Proverbs 26:5 – *"Answer a fool according to his folly, / Lest he be wise in his own conceit."*
    - In fact, in a few verses, Paul is going to give a few characteristics that we are to avoid and in the beginning of Chapter 6, he will talk a little about how to deal with those who practice them.

> The next verse seems to take a little jump. First, we know that Paul *wasn't* teaching circumcision; he's been arguing against it. Yet it seems as though some were claiming that he was and were perhaps even using that claim as part of their own authority to put the Galatians back under the Law.
- Paul, however, argues that if he were indeed preaching circumcision, the resistance and persecution he had endured from the Jewish community should have been over.

- Yet it's clear from Galatians and from 1 Corinthians 7:18-19 that Paul was *not* preaching circumcision: *"Is any man called being circumcised? let him not become uncircumcised. Is any called in uncircumcision? let him not be circumcised. Circumcision is nothing, and uncircumcision is nothing, but the keeping of the commandments of God."*
- And we know the opposition from local Jews never stopped.

➤ Galatians 5:12 looks innocent enough in the English. In fact, "this verse contains what has been called 'the crudest and rudest of all Paul's extant statements.'"[54]

- He's not using "*cut off*" in the sense of isolated or separated from everyone else. The word actually means to chop off or amputate.
- So, what he's saying here is that for those who advocate circumcision, he'd like to see them not stop there, but cut the whole thing off!
  - Note that Deuteronomy 23:1 says: *"He that is wounded in the stones, or hath his privy member cut off, shall not enter into the congregation of the Lord."* So perhaps Paul has a double meaning intended here.

➤ Paul reminds them once again that they are called to liberty but gives them a word of warning as well – do not use that liberty to fall prey to the sins of the flesh. We have heard the same thing in movie slogans: "With great power comes great responsibility." The Galatians had great power in their liberty; they were free from the Law and its restrictions. Yet they could have become so independent, so self-centered in enjoying their freedom through grace that they could have ruined their fellowship and destroyed their witness.

---

54 George, *Galatians*, 371.

- Instead, Paul tells them to love another and to serve one another. He uses the word derived from *doulos* here, or bondservant. So instead of being in bondage to the yoke of the Law, be in bondage to one another in love (*agape*).

➤ Paul reminds them that if they want to fulfill the Law, they should *"love thy neighbour as thyself."* It's the same thing Jesus confirmed to the young man who asked Him what he should do to inherit eternal life (Luke 10:25-28).

➤ What are you in servitude to? In America, we tend to be fiercely independent and hate the idea of bowing the knee to anyone or anything. We do not like to be told what to do, whether it's our boss, our spouse, our government, or our family. Certainly, Americans don't *ever* want other countries to tell us what to do.

- Yet Paul and Jesus tell us we should have the hearts of servants and that we should serve others – not because we're obligated to, not because we are slaves or servants to these masters, but because of our love for Christ and what He has done for us in setting us free.

- Martin Luther put it this way: "A Christian is free and independent in every respect, a bond servant to none. A Christian is a dutiful servant in every respect, owning a duty to everyone."[55]

- When's the last time you were a servant? What was your attitude? Did you resent it? Or were you there hoping to be a blessing to those around you, asking not for recognition or honor, but merely content to work behind the scenes for the good of your friends, family, congregation, or community? Ultimately, we should all be serving our families, our church, and one another. And we should be doing it joyfully.

---

55 George, *Galatians*, 378.

> Likewise, Paul paints the following behavior in contrast – biting and devouring one another. It's not clear if Paul is saying this is an issue or is simply giving a warning, but he uses language applicable to animals.

- We see this in our lives, too. How many times have you said something, even about a fellow believer, only to have what you said come back to you and damage your own reputation? James spends a great deal of time talking about the tongue and how it needs to be tamed.

- Of course, it's not just our words that can hurt, it's also our actions. We can commit sins of commission, but also omission.

- Paul is warning the community that unless they are careful and fulfilling the Law by loving their neighbors, they could very well end up destroying themselves.

 Galatians 5:16-26

16 This I say then, Walk in the Spirit, and ye shall not fulfil the lust of the flesh. 17 For the flesh lusteth against the Spirit, and the Spirit against the flesh: and these are contrary the one to the other: so that ye cannot do the things that ye would. 18 But if ye be led of the Spirit, ye are not under the law. 19 Now the works of the flesh are manifest, which are these; Adultery, fornication, uncleanness, lasciviousness, 20 Idolatry, witchcraft, hatred, variance, emulations, wrath, strife, seditions, heresies, 21 Envyings, murders, drunkenness, revellings, and such like: of the which I tell you before, as I have also told you in time past, that they which do such things shall not inherit the kingdom of God. 22 But the fruit of the Spirit is love, joy, peace, longsuffering, gentleness, goodness, faith, 23 Meekness, temperance: against such there is no law. 24 And they that are Christ's have crucified the flesh with the affections and lusts. 25 If we live in the Spirit, let us also walk in the Spirit. 26 Let us not be desirous of vain glory, provoking one another, envying one another.

- Paul begins this section with a contrast ("*I say then*") to the previous verses about biting and devouring one another.
  - The command: "*Walk in the Spirit*"! An imperative, present tense construction meaning "walk continually in the Spirit!" It's an important enough command that Paul repeats it down in Galatians 5:25.
  - The benefit: *If* you walk in the Spirit, *then* you won't succumb to the lusts of the flesh.
  - Paul's solution is not to rely on a set of rules and regulations (the Law) to ensure good behavior, but to rely on the indwelling of the Spirit.

- Paul presents the Spirit and the flesh as acting in opposition against other. This is our natural state *even when we already have the Spirit* and results in us not doing what we want to do.
  - So, our natural tendency, even once saved, is not to do good or to listen to God. This shouldn't surprise you. Salvation doesn't make us "good." It's been said that "Christ didn't come to make bad men good, but to make dead men live."
  - Even Paul says in Romans 7:15, "*For that which I do I allow not: for what I would, that do I not; but what I hate, that do I.*"

- This sounds simple, but how do we actually *do* it? We know the Galatians received the Spirit because he told us so back in Galatians 3:2.
  - So, our only hope to do what is "good" is to call upon God, to call upon the power of the Spirit to avoid the temptations of the flesh. What are some ways to do this?
    - Pray – certainly, when we're struck by the temptation to sin, we can get on our knees and pray. Paul tells us in 1

Thessalonians 5:16 -18: *"Rejoice evermore. Pray without ceasing. In every thing give thanks: for this is the will of God in Christ Jesus concerning you."*

- Prayer, like a muscle, is something that needs to be exercised. Whether it's saying grace before meals, asking for God's will in guidance, repenting, or just closing the Sunday school class, if we don't pray often enough, that muscle gets weak and atrophies to point where we are too uncomfortable to pray. Practice, practice, practice. Let your kids hear you pray. (How else will they know how to do it?)

    - ✓ Read God's Word – get familiar with what God has to say on various subjects and see, especially in the Proverbs and Prophets, what kind of behavior God expects. *This* is where God "speaks" to us.

    - ✓ Examine your actions – A common Sunday school question is, "If you were arrested for being a Christian, would there be enough evidence to convict you?" Are you walking the talk? Do your actions reflect the character of your King? Are you His ambassador? If not, why not? *This* is where the Spirit convicts us of our behavior.

    - ✓ Be with other Believers – that's not to say you should only surround with other Christ-followers. But if you are not around *anyone* who can help you be accountable, chances are you won't be.

> Paul concludes this section by saying, "If you are led by the Spirit, you are not under the Law."

- As we often do, let's cross out the "if" here and replace it with "because." This is a first class conditional in the Greek where the if-statement is assumed to be true, leading to a true conclusion.
- Paul is telling them that they *are* under the Spirit – hearkening again back to the beginning of Chapter 3 – and saying that the Judaizers have no power over them under the Law. It's a reiteration of Paul's central thesis on grace versus Law.
- To be led by the Law is to be doing works of the flesh.

› In case we don't know what the works of the flesh are, Paul give us quite the catalog:
- Tom Constable in "Tom Constable's Expository Notes on the Bible" groups them into five categories:
  - Sexual
    - Adultery (*moicheia*) – to commit adultery. The act of adultery[56]
    - Fornication (*porneia*) – Any sexual sin; coupled with *moicheía*.[57] Symbolically it stands for idolatry, the forsaking of the true God in order to worship idols.[58]
    - Uncleanness (*akatharsia*) – unclean. Uncleanness or filth in a natural or physical sense (Matt. 23:27; Septuagint: 2 Sam. 11:4); moral uncleanness, lewdness, incontinence in general (Rom. 6:19; Eph. 4:19; 5:3; 1 Thess. 2:3 of avarice; Thess. 4:7); any kind of uncleanness different from whoredom (2 Cor. 12:21); any unnatural pollution, whether acted out by oneself (Gal. 5:19; Col. 3:5), or

---

56 Zodhiates, *The complete word study dictionary: New Testament.*
57 Ibid.
58 Ibid.

with another (Rom. 1:24 [cf. Rom. 1:26, 27]; Septuagint: Ezek. 22:15; 36:25).[59]

- Lewdness (*aselgeia*)-- Lasciviousness, license, debauchery, sexual excess, absence of restraint, insatiable desire for pleasure.[60]

○ Religious

- Idolatry (*idololatreia*) – Idolatry

- Sorcery (*pharmakeia*) -- a drug, which in the Greek is used both for a curative or medicinal drug, and also as a poisonous one. *Pharmakeía* means the occult, sorcery, witchcraft, illicit pharmaceuticals, trance, magical incantation with drugs[61]

○ Societal

- Enmities (*ecthra*) -- Enmity, hatred, hostility

- Strife (*eris*) -- Strife, contention, wrangling (Rom. 13:13; 1 Cor. 1:11; 3:3; 2 Cor. 12:20; Gal. 5:20; 1 Tim. 6:4; Titus 3:9); acc. *érin* (Phil 1:15), pl. *érides* (1 Cor. 1:11) / *éreis* (2 Cor. 12:20). Metaphorically, it means love of strife (Rom. 1:29; Phil. 1:15).[62]

- Jealousy (*zelos*) - Zeal, used in a good sense (John 2:17; Rom. 10:2; 2 Cor. 7:7, 11; 11:2; Col. 4:13; Sept.: Ps. 69:9; 119:139) and more often in an evil sense, meaning envy, jealousy, anger[63]

---

59 Ibid.
60 Ibid.
61 Ibid.
62 Ibid.
63 Ibid.

- Indignations (*thumos*) - masculine noun from *thúō* (n.f.), to move impetuously, particularly as the air or wind, a violent motion or passion of the mind. Anger, wrath, indignation[64] This can be described as an anger that erupts.

- Contentions (*eritheia*) - from *eritheúō* (n.f.), to work for hire, usually in the middle voice, used in a bad sense of those who seek only their own. Contention, strife, rivalry. It represents a motive of self-interest, mercenary interest (Phil. 1:16; 2:3). It also meant canvassing for public office, scheming. (Rom. 2:8; 2 Cor. 12:20; Gal. 5:20; James 3:14, 16.)[65]

- Divisions (*dichostasia*) - from *dícha* (n.f.), separately, and *stásis* (4714), dissension. A separate faction, division, separation (Rom. 16:17; 1 Cor. 3:3; Gal. 5:20).[66]

- Heresies (*hairesis*) - noun from *hairéō* (138), to choose, select. Heresy, a form of religious worship, discipline, or opinion (Acts 5:17; 15:5; 24:5, 14; 26:5; 28:22; 1 Cor. 11:19; Gal. 5:20; 2 Pet. 2:1). In contrast to *schísma* (4978), schism which is an actual tearing apart, *haíresis* may represent a divergent opinion but still be part of a whole. One can hold different views than the majority and remain in the same body, but he is a heretic (*hairetikós* [141]). However, when he tears himself away (*schízō* [4977]), then he is schismatic. Heresy may lead to schism which is when actual tearing off and separation occur.[67]

---

64 Ibid.
65 Ibid.
66 Ibid.
67 Ibid.

- Envyings (*pthonos*) - Envy, jealousy, pain felt and malignity conceived at the sight of excellence or happiness[68]
- Murders (*phonos*) - Murder, particularly slaughter, slaying or killing by the sword[69]

○ Uncontrolled

- Drunkennesses (*methe*) - from *méthu* (n.f., see below), milled wine. Drunkenness (Luke 21:34; Rom. 13:13; Gal. 5:21; Septuagint: Ezek. 23:32; 39:19). **Deriv.** of *méthu* (n.f.): *methúskō* (3182), to make or become drunk; *méthusos* (3183), a drunkard; *methúō* (3184), to be drunk.[70]
- Revels (*komos*) - A feasting, used in the plural only in the New Testament meaning riotous conduct (Rom. 13:13); revellings (Gal. 5:21; 1 Pet. 4:3); festivities in honor of several gods, especially Bacchus, the god of wine, hence feastings and drunkenness with impurity and obscenity of the grossest kind. Therefore, it always presupposes a festive company and drunken revelers.[71]

○ "*and such like*"

- Evidently Paul's catch-all category of things offensive to God

➤ Paul now gives us a forewarning (*prolego*-to say before) about a key topic.

---

68 Ibid.
69 Ibid.
70 Ibid.
71 Ibid.

- He tells that those who "*do*" (*prasso*-in the present tense, to do continually or by habit) will not "*inherit*" the "*kingdom of God.*"[72]

- What are we to make of this? I thought that if you were a Christian who had placed his faith in Christ, your sins were forgiven – even future sins? Are we saying that those who profess to be Christians, but do these things are not saved? That they are unbelievers?

- Let's look at another inheritance passage, 1 Corinthians 6:9-11:

  > 9 Know ye not that the unrighteous shall not inherit the kingdom of God? Be not deceived: neither fornicators, nor idolaters, nor adulterers, nor effeminate, nor abusers of themselves with mankind, 10 Nor thieves, nor covetous, nor drunkards, nor revilers, nor extortioners, shall inherit the kingdom of God. 11 And such were some of you: but ye are washed, but ye are sanctified, but ye are justified in the name of the Lord Jesus, and by the Spirit of our God.

- Or what about this in Ephesians 1:11? It states: "*In whom also we have obtained an inheritance, being predestinated according to the purpose of him who worketh all things after the counsel of his own will.*"

  o What do we do with these verses?

  o First, I think it's clear from Scripture that "*For whosoever shall call upon the name of the Lord shall be saved*" (Rom. 10:13).

    • "*Whosoever.*" There is no fine print that excludes certain classes of sinner, no matter how bad the sinner is.

---

72 THE KINGDOM OF GOD IS A DIFFICULT SUBJECT WHICH REQUIRES ADDITIONAL STUDY. IF YOU ARE TEACHING THROUGH GALATIANS AND HAVE NOT HAD AT LEAST SOME INTRODUCTION TO A DISPENSATIONAL VIEW OF THE KINGDOM AS A TRUE, PHYSICAL, LITERAL KINGDOM OFFERED TO THE JEWS (**NOT** THE CHURCH) DURING THE PERIOD OF THE GOSPELS, I URGE YOU TO TAKE ON THAT STUDY. THE KINGDOM IS NOT GOD "REIGNING IN MEN'S HEARTS," NOR ARE CHRISTIANS "DOING KINGDOM WORK."

- ♦ Thus, we should be comfortable in this current Age of Grace that Christians are "*saved.*" The only way we could apply this to Christians is if we believe that it's possible to lose your salvation. In other words, we would have to adopt an Armenian viewpoint where we step in and out of being saved by our actions. However, since we are saved as a result of *His* faithfulness, not ours, I do not subscribe to the Armenian view.
- The question, then, is who does the Kingdom apply to? And who would therefore inherit it?
  - First, the Kingdom applies to the Jew. It's a Jewish promise. A development of the concept of the Kingdom is beyond the scope of this study, however as early as Exodus 19:6, Moses is told to tell the newly called nation of Israel: "*And ye shall be unto me a kingdom of priests, and an holy nation. These are the words which thou shalt speak unto the children of Israel.*" Here, the concept of the Kingdom is introduced.
  - Psalm 22:28 says, "*For the kingdom is the LORD's: / And he is the governor among the nations.*"
  - Psalm 145:13 speaks of God's kingdom as an "*everlasting kingdom.*"
  - Isaiah 9:7, speaking of Jesus, tells us:

    Of the increase of his government and peace there shall be no end,

    Upon the throne of David, and upon his kingdom,

    To order it, and to establish it with judgment and with justice

    From henceforth even for ever.

    The zeal of the Lord of hosts will perform this

- And in Matthew 3:2, Jesus tells us, *"And saying, Repent ye: for the kingdom of heaven is at hand."*
- The Kingdom is a real, physical kingdom that must be future because Jesus has never sat upon David's throne.

- What about inheriting?
  - Inheritance as a concept is tied to the land of Israel as far back as Genesis and God's promise to Abram in Genesis 15:7: *"And he said unto him, I am the LORD that brought thee out of Ur of the Chaldees, to give thee this land to inherit it."*
  - God reaffirmed the promise in Exodus 32:13: *"Remember Abraham, Isaac, and Israel, thy servants, to whom thou swarest by thine own self, and sadist unto them, I will multiply your seed as the stars of heaven, and all this land that I have spoken of will I give unto your seed, and they shall inherit it for ever."*
  - In one of His parables, Jesus tells His disciples: *"Then shall the King say unto them on his right hand, Come, ye blessed of my father, inherit the kingdom prepared for you from the foundation of the world."* (Matt. 25:34).
  - Who are the *"blessed of my Father"*? Not the church – the Jew. In fact, in the Gospels, inheritance was a key question asked of Jesus:
    - Mark 10:17 – *"And when he was gone forth into the way, there came one running, and kneeled to him, and asked him, Good Master, what shall I do that I may inherit eternal life?"*
    - Luke 10:25 – *"And, behold, a certain lawyer stood up, and tempted him, saying, Master, what shall I do to inherit eternal life?"*
    - Luke 18:18 – *"And a certain ruler asked him, saying, Good Master, what shall I do to inherit eternal life?"*

- So, the Jew associated land with the inheritance with eternal life.
- Therefore, if **Inheritance is a Jewish issue** and that's what he associated with the land and eternal life, AND Christians are saved by calling on the Lord, **then there's actually nothing to *inherit* for the Christian.**
    - Furthermore, who are the "*predestined*" in Ephesians? Again, we can't develop this within the Galatians study, but there is only one "chosen," "predestined," or "elect" people – the Israelites. If you are a Christian, you are **not** one of the elect (unless you declare yourself as a Calvinist).
    - So, if that's true, why is Paul writing about inheritance in these passages?
    - Because Paul is talking to congregations at Corinth, Galatia, and Ephesus which were all heavily Jewish, and he is writing to the Jews in particular within those congregations.
    - If we are to accept this viewpoint (from a dispensational perspective, it makes sense), then this warning is being applied to the Judaizers and possibly to Gentile converts who would fall back on saying that they had kept the Law (or elements of it like circumcision) thinking they were proselytes yet had in fact broken the Law and did so continually.
    - Thus, Paul would not be saying to those under Grace, "You will lose your salvation," or more accurately, "your justification through your faith in the blood of Christ." Instead, this warning continues to fit within the framework of those would seek to find salvation through works.

> Paul contrasts the works of the flesh with the fruit of the Spirit (implying that we will recognize works that flow from this fruit).
> - Love (*agape*) – noun from *agapáō* (25), to love. Love, affectionate regard, goodwill, benevolence. With reference to God's love, it is God's willful direction toward man. It involves God doing what He knows is best for man and not necessarily what man desires[73]
> - Joy (*chara*) – noun from *chairō* (5463), to rejoice. Joy, rejoicing, gladness.[74]
> - Peace (*eirene*) – Particularly in a single sense, the opposite of war and dissension (Luke 14:32; Acts 12:20; Rev. 6:4). Among individuals, peace, harmony[75]
> - Patience/long-suffering (*makrothumia*) – noun from *makrothuméō* (3114), to be long-suffering. Forbearance, long-suffering, self-restraint before proceeding to action. The quality of a person who is able to avenge himself yet refrains from doing so[76]
> - Kindness (*chrestotes*) – noun from *chrēstós* (5543), useful, profitable. Benignity, kindness, usefulness. It often occurs with *philanthrōpía* (5363), philanthropy; *anochḗ* (463), forbearance (Rom. 2:4), and is the opposite of *apotomía* (663), severity or cutting something short and quickly (Rom. 11:22). *Chrēstótēs* is translated "good" (Rom. 3:12); "kindness" (2 Cor. 6:6; Eph. 2:7; Col. 3:12; Titus 3:4); "gentleness" (Gal. 5:22). It is the grace which pervades the whole nature, mellowing all which would be been harsh and austere. Thus, wine is *chrēstós* (5543), mellowed with age (Luke 5:39). The word is descriptive of one's disposition

---

[73] Zodhiates, *The complete word study dictionary: New Testament.*
[74] Ibid.
[75] Ibid.
[76] Ibid.

and does not necessarily entail acts of goodness as does the word *agathōsúnē* (19), active benignity. *Chrēstótēs* has the harmlessness of the dove but not the wisdom of the serpent which *agathōsúnē* shows in sharpness and rebuke.[77]

- Goodness (*agathosune*) – noun from *agathós* (18), benevolent. Active goodness.[78] Beneficence, in Galatians 5:22 referred to as goodness, but the English word includes several pleasing qualities whereas the Greek word refers to one particular quality. It is more than *chrēstótēs* (5544), gentleness, kindness, a mellowing of character. It is character energized, expressing itself in *agathón* (18), benevolence, active good. There is more activity in *agathōsúnē* than in *chrēstótēs*. *Agathōsúnē* does not spare sharpness and rebuke to cause good (*agathón*) in others. A person may display his *agathōsúnē*, his zeal for goodness and truth, in rebuking, correcting, or chastising. Christ's righteous indignation in the temple (Matt. 21:13) showed His *agathōsúnē*, goodness, but not His *chrēstótēs*, gentleness. See Romans 15:14; Ephephesians 5:9; 2 Thessalonians 1:11.[79]

- Faith [not really faithfulness (-correct in the YLT)] (*pistis*) – noun from *peíthō* (3982), to win over, persuade. Faith. Subjectively meaning firm persuasion, conviction, belief in the truth, veracity, reality or faithfulness (though rare). Objectively meaning that which is believed, doctrine, the received articles of faith[80] (So it seems that *faith* or improved/increasing faith is a result of the fruit of the Spirit, not an increase in faithfulness as a believer. This is perhaps a subtle point.)

---

77 Ibid.
78 Ibid.
79 Ibid.
80 Ibid.

- Meekness (*praotes*) – noun from *práos* (4235), meek. Meekness, mildness, forbearance (1 Cor. 4:21; 2 Cor. 10:1; Gal. 5:23; 6:1; Eph. 4:2; Col. 3:12; 1 Tim. 6:11; 2 Tim. 2:25; Titus 3:2; Sept.: Ps. 45:6). Primarily, it does not denote outward expression of feeling, but an inward grace of the soul, calmness toward God in particular. It is the acceptance of God's dealings with us considering them as good in that they enhance the closeness of our relationship with Him.[81] (This is not a virtue from a Greek or Roman perspective.) This meekness does not blame God for the persecutions and evil doings of men. It is not the result of weakness, and in the third Beatitude it expresses not the passivity of the second Beatitude, but the activity of the blessedness that exists in one's heart from being actively angry at evil. According to Aristotle, *praótēs* is that virtue that stands between two extremes, the *orgilótēs* (n.f.), uncontrolled and unjustified anger (see *orgílos* [3711], quickly angry), and *aorgisía* (n.f.), not becoming angry at all no matter what takes place around you.[82]

- Self-control (*egkrateia*) – noun from *egkratḗs* (1468), temperate, self–controlled. Continence, temperance, self–control[83]

- We all know this verse. We can sing about what fruits the Spirit are not. But how are you doing on demonstrating these – particularly in these turbulent times?

➤ *"Against such, there is no Law."* I think this means either, "the Law cannot stand" or "the Law is clearly inferior."

➤ Verse 24 is interesting.

- Back in Galatians 2:20, Paul wrote, *"I am crucified with Christ…"*

---

81 Ibid.
82 Ibid.
83 Ibid.

This language uses the same verb root, but a different form. In 2:20, crucifixion acted on Paul – he did not do anything. In this verse, the verb is active, meaning that it is the believer who does the crucifying.

- We (believers) have *"crucified the flesh"* with all of its passions. We do not need to subject to it any more.
- Why? Because (again, strike the 'if' and replace it) we live by the Spirit (not the Law). And here Paul once again exhorts us to walk by the Spirit. To live out our faith.

> He concludes with an admonition against behavior that must have been within the Galatian church:

- Vainglorious (*kenodoxos*) – adjective from *kenós* (2756), empty or vain, and *dóxa* (1391), glory or praise. It denotes a person who is void of real worth but who wants to be admired by others [84]
- Provoking (*prokaleo*) – from *pró* (4253), forward, and *kaléō* (2564), to call. Used in the middle to refer to calling before oneself, i.e., to challenge, provoke, irritate, with the accusative (Gal. 5:26).[85]
- Envying (*phthoneo*) – to envy

We're guilty of that behavior ourselves. Often. Even the most devout Christian can be irritating or jealous of someone or something. Many times, we don't even realize we are doing it, but if we would *"walk by the Spirit,"* we could recognize and correct that behavior.

---

84 Ibid.

85 Ibid.

CONCLUSION

- There was a lot to unpack in Chapter 5 as Paul began to transition from a strict persuasive argument about the benefits of Grace vs. Law to more practical application. Yet he never let the matter go completely.

- The key thoughts for us?
  - Liberty – Recognize the liberty we have in Christ to live as Paul would, not as subjects under the Law nor dependent upon it for our own justification.
  - Walk in the Spirit – given our Liberty, the believer should listen for the Spirit to guide him and enjoy the results, the fruit.
    - If you are a believer, but the fruits are not evident in your life (and they likely won't be all the time), then you are probably not walking by the Spirit. It should be a bit of a wake-up call.
    - As you become more mature in your faith (not just more knowledgeable about the Bible but doing the things we outlined earlier to understand who God is, what His word says, what He expects of us), then the fruits should manifest themselves more often.
  - We spent a good deal of time going through definitions – the goal was that when you see these words, you think back to the ancient definition, not the modern one, because sometimes the usage is not the same.

- In chapter 6, Paul will continue to tell us how to behave as believers.

GALATIANS CHAPTER 6

INTRODUCTION

➤ As Paul closed Chapter 5, he urged the Galatians to "*walk in the Spirit*" demonstrating the fruits of the Spirit to other Believers. He's become a "kinder, gentler" Paul as he prepares to close his letter.

➤ Chapter 6 continues in this same vein – Paul giving advice on how to live in this mixed Gentile and Jewish community that was Galatia. "No more back-biting! No more putting yourself above another brother!"

➤ If you are in Christ, you have crucified the flesh with its worldly passions and desires (Gal. 5:24).

- Of course, we know that is easier said than done. Just because we have accepted Christ, does not mean that we actually *are* kinder or gentler. The network news, that colleague in the office, that guy who cut you off on the road – all of these can take away from our peace and prevent us from displaying the outward fruit of the inward Spirit.

➤ Paul will remind the Galatians of this as he talks about the brother who is caught up in sin and how those around him should deal with him.

LESSON

 Galatians 6:1-5

> 6 Brethren, if a man be overtaken in a fault, ye which are spiritual, restore such an one in the spirit of meekness; considering thyself, lest thou also be tempted. 2 Bear ye one another's burdens, and so fulfil the law of Christ. 3 For if a man think himself to be something, when he is nothing, he deceiveth himself. 4 But let every man prove his own work, and then shall he have rejoicing in himself alone, and not in another. 5 For every man shall bear his own burden.

➤ Paul reverts to calling the Galatians "*Brethren*," or in the Greek, *adelphoi*. This suggests that words which follow are not necessarily meant as condemnation or scolding but as gentle encouragement in dealing with issues that Paul knows must be present.

➤ Let's establish the situation for Paul's advice in Galatians 5:1:

- "*if a man be overtaken in a fault*"
    - What does this mean?
    - In Greek, the language is: "if even a man be overtaken."
        - Many times, I have suggested that you cross out an 'if' and replace it with a 'since' or 'because.' This is *not* one of those times. Paul is not saying that this situation has occurred. Instead, he is raising the possibility that it could occur and is giving advice on what to do if it does.
        - What does it mean to be "*overtaken*"?
            - ✓ The word is *prolambino*, from *pro* (before) and *lambano* (to take). So literally, to take before. Some of your translations may translate this as "caught"

and that is reasonable – the dictionaries agree that there is an element of *surprise* here – that the brother in question is either surprised because he has been discovered committing the sin or that he is surprised himself to be committing the sin and to have others point it out.

- ✓ Some commentators suggest there is the idea of a runner being overtaken in a race from behind and being surprised by it.
- ✓ Have you ever been overtaken in sin? My guess is yes. There are times when we sin before we even know it and when someone points it out to us, we are surprised and hopefully, a bit embarrassed.

- ◆ The "*fault*" is an offense, a falling by the wayside.

➤ Let's find out how to deal with this:
- "*ye which are spiritual*" – some commentators have read sarcasm into this address, mocking those who wanted to reinvigorate the Law within the congregation.
- I think, however, with Paul's tender opening of "*Brethren*," that Paul is really urging those among them who are more spiritually mature.
- "*Restore*" the brother at fault – the word *katartizo* means to put back in the right condition. It was used of mending the fishing nets in the Gospels (Matt. 4:21, Mark 1:19). It was also the same word for setting a broken bone.
- What attitude should the "restorer" have? Gentleness, or as we have seen in the previous chapter and in the King James Version, "*meekness.*" We should not beat the person over the head with their mistake but rather restore his behavior calmly and directly.

- By the way, I think this example of *"a man,"* in context, is really a man within the fellowship. I don't think Paul is necessarily talking about an unbeliever (Why would he be surprised to be caught up in sin or even acknowledge it as such?).

➤ Paul gives us a warning at the end of this instruction – do your correcting with an eye to yourself (*skopeo*-to spy out or mark) because you might also be tempted.

- Tempted by what is not clear – presumably the same sin that you are correcting. But one could also see this as tempted to lord your spirituality over the person you are correcting.

- Paul has already warned that a little leaven leavens the whole lump, so it makes sense in that context that Paul is telling how this sin must be confronted before it has a chance to spread and that the one it could spread to first is the one trying to do the correcting.

- It's not clear if there is a specific example that Paul has in mind. However, to look for such an example of how Paul responded, look to 1 Corinthians 5. Here, there was an adulterer in the midst of the congregation and rather than addressing it, Paul says they were *"puffed up"* about it:

    > *5 It is reported commonly that there is fornication among you, and such fornication as is not so much as named among the Gentiles, that one should have his father's wife.* **2 And ye are puffed up, and have not rather mourned, that he that hath done this deed might be taken away from among you.** *3 For I verily, as absent in body, but present in spirit, have judged already, as though I were present, concerning him that hath so done this deed, 4 In the name of our Lord Jesus Christ, when ye are gathered together, and my spirit, with the power of our Lord Jesus Christ, 5 To deliver such an one unto Satan for the destruction of the flesh, that the spirit may be saved in the day of the Lord Jesus. 6 Your glorying is not good. Know ye not that a little leaven leaveneth the whole lump? 7 Purge out therefore the old leaven, that ye may be a new lump,*

> *as ye are unleavened. For even Christ our passover is sacrificed for us: 8 Therefore let us keep the feast, not with old leaven, neither with the leaven of malice and wickedness; but with the unleavened bread of sincerity and truth.*
>
> *9 I wrote unto you in an epistle not to company with fornicators: 10 Yet not altogether with the fornicators of this world, or with the covetous, or extortioners, or with idolaters; for then must ye needs go out of the world. 11 But now I have written unto you not to keep company, if any man that is called a brother be a fornicator, or covetous, or an idolater, or a railer, or a drunkard, or an extortioner; with such an one no not to eat. 12 For what have I to do to judge them also that are without? do not ye judge them that are within? 13 But them that are without God judgeth. Therefore put away from among yourselves that wicked person.*[86]

- The situation in Corinth was serious. And it implied an ongoing action which was well-known by the congregation. Paul urged them as a congregation to deal with it and to remove the man in question from fellowship until the behavior was restored. We learn in 2 Corinthians 2:5-8 that this man was ultimately reconciled back to the fellowship.

- How do we apply this? I think it has become very difficult for us as the church and as individual believers to address behavioral issues like this. On the one hand, we might ask ourselves whether it's our business. Are we our brother's keeper? (And I think we have a scriptural answer on that.) Doesn't God love everyone? (Yes, but is He is also a holy, righteous, and just God.) But I don't have any proof! (Then it is probably best to hold your tongue.) But won't it damage the fellowship, with him/her and within the congregation? (Probably, particularly if a congregation is reluctant to deal with things out in the open.) But what about mercy? (Mercy is given to those who are repentant, not to those consistently involved in sins like Paul describes.)

---

86 emphasis added

- It's a difficult issue, but Paul is here ultimately concerned with restoring that believer who has sinned, who acknowledges it, and repents.

▸ But how do we balance this discussion of helping a brother or sister get back on the right path, sometimes, through hard discipline, with our outreach to the unsaved? Won't that turn those who are not saved away from the church as they look at us being judgmental or legalistic?

- I think one key lies in Paul's comments in 1 Corinthians 5:12. The discussion about correcting behavior and perhaps having to put someone out of the church is for those *in* the church. It is meant to help a fellow believer walk in the Spirit and to turn away from sin, again in gentleness, but it is a serious charge for us. Often in the church, we either tolerate everything or we tolerate nothing. One extreme ignores God's holy, righteous nature and the other extreme forgets God's grace (and the fact that we are all sinners).

- On the other hand, we must reach out to the unsaved and we shouldn't expect their behavior to line up with what we would expect of a Christian. Sometimes we are surprised that someone comes into the church and is not instantly transformed. Yet Paul reminds us that we are a work in progress (Phil. 1:6) and that in the case of the new Christian, God may be starting that work from scratch. He has done that with some of us, too.

- So, while we should condemn sin, we should not be so zealous (or indeed prideful) that we could be responsible for someone turning away from salvation. Rather, let us bring the sinner to Christ and then do what Jesus commanded in Matthew 28:19 – "*Go and make disciples…*" (One might argue that this applied only to the Twelve Disciples and not to us, but I believe there are ample examples in Paul's writings which would absolutely apply to the church.)

- As the church, our work does not stop when someone comes to Christ, it must continue to help new believers (and not so new) continue to mature in Christ.

➤ Getting back to believers inside the church, let me suggest this model for correction:
- First, as an individual, have a mentor/accountability partner. Read the scripture together and confess your sins to one another. Build trust. Pray.
- If you do not have that relationship, or you find that your partner is not responsive to your guidance, then you should be continually in prayer, but your next step is to follow the model of corporate church discipline laid out by Jesus in Matthew 18:15-17.
- This could be difficult and uncomfortable, but remember as we have just seen, it is what Paul prescribed, and the man in question was ultimately restored to the fellowship.

➤ *"Bear ye one another's burdens,"*
- The word for burden here is *baros*, a heavy, difficult load to carry.
- This is another command and one that is designed not only to lighten our own induvial loads, but to build fellowship.
- We all have burdens. Some are obvious, but some are buried. One purpose of Life Groups, Bible study groups, and Sunday School classes is to know each other well enough that we know about these burdens and that we actively take on the sharing of them.
  - We are all busy; sometimes our own burdens are so great that we don't even notice the ones of those around us. Yet have you ever found that lifting the burden of another, even in the midst of your own, can bring you relief, satisfaction, or joy?

- What, then, is the law of Christ? I think it refers back up to Galatians 5:14 – *"For all the law is fulfilled in one word, even in this: 'You shall love your neighbor as yourself.'"*[87]

> This next verse is a great one: Don't think too much of yourself; you are not "all that."

- Don't be conceited. Paul's emphasis is on thinking that you are better than others or that you are something special.
- Yet in thinking that, he tells us that we deceive ourselves. Don't let that leaven into your own thinking.

> Instead, look to your own work and "test" for approval – is it worthy?

- Likewise, our yardstick is not other believers or other churches as Paul tells in 2 Corinthians 10:12: *"For we dare not make ourselves of the number, or compare ourselves with some that commend themselves: but they measuring themselves by themselves, and comparing themselves among themselves, are not wise."*
- And continuing in 2 Corinthians 10:17-18: *"But he that glorieth, let him glory in the Lord. For not he that commendeth himself is approved, but whom the Lord commendeth."*
- Boasting in oneself carries with it the idea that you have evaluated your work and believe it worthy. It's a little strange that Paul talks about not being prideful, but then talks about boasting because of works done.
  - First, I think Paul may be looking ahead to Galatians 6:13-14 where the Judaizers would boast that they caused these Gentiles to become circumcised, yet Paul would boast about the cross – different kinds of boasting, different kind of focus.

---

87 *New King James Version*; emphasis added

> Doesn't Galatians 6:5 look like it contradicts what we just saw a few verses earlier? The New American Commentary helps to resolve the situation:

> This apparent discrepancy is easily resolved when we realize that Paul was using two different words to refer to two disparate situations. The word translated "burdens" in v. 2 (*barē*) refers, as we have seen, to a heavy load, an oppressive weight, which one is expected to carry for a long distance. But the word for "load" in v. 5 is *phortion*, which is used elsewhere to refer to a ship's cargo (cf. Acts 27:10), a soldier's knapsack, or a pilgrim's backpack.[88]

- J. Stott correctly delineates the difference between the two "loads" in Galatians 6:

> "So we are to bear one another's 'burdens' which are too heavy for a man to bear alone, but there is one burden which we cannot share—indeed do not need to because it is a pack light enough for every man to carry himself—and that is our responsibility to God on the day of judgment. On that day you cannot carry my pack and I cannot carry yours."[89]

---

88 Moffatt translates this verse, "Everyone will have to bear his own load of responsibility." Burton correctly notes that no sharp distinction can be drawn between these two words as such (*Galatians*, 334). However, the context in Gal 6 clearly shows that Paul had two distinct meanings in mind.

89 George, *Galatians*, 418.

Galatians 6:6-10

> *6 Let him that is taught in the word communicate unto him that teacheth in all good things. 7 Be not deceived; God is not mocked: for whatsoever a man soweth, that shall he also reap. 8 For he that soweth to his flesh shall of the flesh reap corruption; but he that soweth to the Spirit shall of the Spirit reap life everlasting. 9 And let us not be weary in well doing: for in due season we shall reap, if we faint not. 10 As we have therefore opportunity, let us do good unto all men, especially unto them who are of the household of faith.*

- The teaching on supporting the teacher seems a bit random. However, it is possible that in the context of the verses of bearing one another's burdens directly above, there has been a disagreement or a discontinuation of support for a local teacher. Perhaps this arose out the Judaizers conflict with that teacher, or perhaps it was simply selfishness or neglect.
  - I also wonder whether it could be that these believers have failed to support Paul? Paul typically tried to ensure that he was no burden to any local church:
    - 2 Corinthians 11:9 – *"And when I was present with you, and wanted, I was chargeable to no man: for that which was lacking to me the brethren which came from Macedonia supplied: and in all things I have kept myself from being burdensome unto you, and so will I keep myself."*
    - 1 Thessalonians 2:9 – *"For ye remember, brethren, our labour and travail: for labouring night and day, because we would not be chargeable unto any of you, we preached unto you the gospel of God."*

- He supported himself through his work as a tent maker, though he sometimes did receive donations and for those, he was grateful.
- Nevertheless, he did assert his right to paid for his labors and for the church to pay its pastors. In 1 Corinthians 9:8-15, Paul writes:

  > *8 Say I these things as a man? or saith not the law the same also? 9 For it is written in the law of Moses, Thou shalt not muzzle the mouth of the ox that treadeth out the corn. Doth God take care for oxen? 10 Or saith he it altogether for our sakes? For our sakes, no doubt, this is written: that he that ploweth should plow in hope; and that he that thresheth in hope should be partaker of his hope. 11 If we have sown unto you spiritual things, is it a great thing if we shall reap your carnal things? 12 If others be partakers of this power over you, are not we rather? Nevertheless we have not used this power; but suffer all things, lest we should hinder the gospel of Christ. 13 Do ye not know that they which minister about holy things live of the things of the temple? and they which wait at the altar are partakers with the altar? 14 Even so hath the Lord ordained that they which preach the gospel should live of the gospel. 15 But I have used none of these things: neither have I written these things, that it should be so done unto me: for it were better for me to die, than that any man should make my glorying void.*

- But Paul does believe the teachers should be supported.
  - To share is to be a partaker – from *koinoneo* – the same word we use to describe fellowship.
  - The one who teaches is the *katechounti* and the ones taught are the *katechoumenos*.
    - Both come from the same word, *katecheo*, which is derived from *kata*, an intensifier to the ultimate degree, and *echeo*, to sound (echo). Thus, to be *katecheo* is to be thoroughly instructed.

- It is the word from which we get catechism. We don't call formal instruction in the Baptist church by that name, but in we certainly see it in Catholicism as well as other mainline Protestant denominations including Lutherans and Methodists.

> From encouraging the Galatians to support their teachers, Paul now warns them of the consequences of not doing so. There are three elements to what Paul is saying:

- *"Be not deceived;"*
  - Imperative tense – a command
  - Literally – to be led astray
  - Do we sometimes deceive ourselves about God? I think we do. Hearkening back to the earlier discussion about God being a loving God versus God being judge, we can go to the extreme of not believing that God will judge sin. Consider former pastor Rob Bell who writes in his book *Love Wins*, that despite it being clear in the Bible, there is no hell. He has definitely been deceived.
  - Don't let yourself become deceived. Understand what God's Word says!

- *God is not mocked*:
  - The word comes from *muktērízō*; future *muktērísō*, from *muktḗr* (n.f.), the nose, nostril, which is from *músso* (n.f.), to clear away mucus (*múxa* [n.f.]) by blowing. To turn up one's nose in scorn and hence to mock, deride (Gal. 6:7, meaning God will not let Himself be mocked; see Septuagint Job 22:19; Ps. 80:6).[90]

---

90 Zodhiates, *The complete word study dictionary: New Testament.*

- This is not to say that people do not mock God today – but in the context of the verse as it continues, it is saying that there will be consequences to mocking God. In other words, "Don't kid yourselves, you can't turn your nose up at God with no consequence."

- *"for whatsoever a man soweth, that shall he also reap."*
  - This is not an uncommon saying – we harvest what we plant.
  - In Hosea 8:7, we hear much the same warning: *"They sow the wind, And reap the whirlwind."*[91]
  - When we sow tomato seeds in the ground, we don't get watermelons. We get tomatoes. Thus, it is with our own actions. There is still grace for the believer, but there are consequences to our actions.

- We can probably look at this verse in a broader context, expanding it just from the discussion of supporting teachers to the context of the broader command to walk in the Spirit, enjoy the fruit of the spirit, and the command to bear one another's burdens.

- Paul expands his warning:
  - *"For he that soweth to his flesh shall of the flesh reap corruption"*
    - First, that word *"for"* could be translated as "because;" it is the idea that the previous is causal to what follows.
    - That's pretty self-explanatory. Here, flesh is *sarx*, which can simply mean the flesh of your body or an animal's body, or it can imply, as I think it does in this verse, a carnality as our actions are considered.
    - It may also be referring to relying on works, rather than Spirit as Paul contrasts it with the Spirit next.

---

91 *New King James Version.*

- Corruption is *phthora*, a word we encountered in Chapter 5, and means corruption, but also spoiling, destruction, etc.
- Jesus gives a similar warning to Peter when he tells him in Matthew 26:52 – *"But Jesus said to him, 'Put your sword in its place, for all who take the sword will perish by the sword.'"*
- I wonder if Paul has a double meaning here in this warning:
  - ✓ First, in the obvious context, of bearing one another's burdens and supporting the local teacher;
  - ✓ But it may also fit to say he is continuing on with his larger theme of Grace versus Law and reminding once again that if you want to be judged by your works, it will lead to destruction.
- In 2 Corinthians 9:6, Paul flips this warning around, reminding the Corinthians of the blessings that can come from reaping what is properly sown. This verse, too, is in the context of gifts to the local church: *"But this I say, He which soweth sparingly shall also reap sparingly; and he which soweth bountifully shall reap also bountifully."*

○ In contrast to sewing by the flesh, those *"that soweth to the Spirit shall of the Spirit reap life everlasting."*

- Paul is not just talking about doing things. We could certainly say that we can reap good things when we take care to sow good things.
- But Paul is referring to sowing *"to"* the Spirit. The Greek preposition means "towards, or in the direction of." So, we are taking action in line with the Spirit.

- In the movie *Gladiator*, Maximus the Roman general, tells his men before battle, "What we do in life echoes in eternity." Does that not apply to our decision whether to accept to Christ? Whether to sow to the Spirit?

> It's frustrating, though, isn't it, to consider this verse and see those around us sowing but not reaping the consequences. Often, we hear people talk about "karma," which includes the idea of sowing and reaping that we are discussing here or more commonly that "what comes around, goes around."

- Yet, sometimes it doesn't seem as though it goes around fast enough. If course, we are looking at it from the perspective of wanting judgement for others based on their behavior (while relying on grace for our own behaviors!).
- There will of course be a final judgment when all will reap what they have sown, either to destruction or eternal life – remember that as you consider whether you have believed in Christ or not!
- Peter tells us in 2 Peter 3:3-7:

> *3 Knowing this first, that there shall come in the last days scoffers, walking after their own lusts, 4 And saying, Where is the promise of his coming? for since the fathers fell asleep, all things continue as they were from the beginning of the creation. 5 For this they willingly are ignorant of, that by the word of God the heavens were of old, and the earth standing out of the water and in the water: 6 Whereby the world that then was, being overflowed with water, perished: 7 But the heavens and the earth, which are now, by the same word are kept in store, reserved unto fire against the day of judgment and perdition of ungodly men.*

> Those who sow in the flesh will ultimately reap their reward.

> Yet Paul encourages us to not give up. Don't grow weary of doing good!

- And we do grow weary sometimes, don't we? We see all that's going on in the world around us and sometimes we wonder, why bother? Why try to make a difference?
- Young's literal translation says: *"and in the doing good we may not be faint-hearted, for at the proper time we shall reap—not desponding."*[92]
  - Let's unpack this:
    - *"Doing good"* – in the present tense implying a continuous action – to continually be doing things which are of good quality and character
    - *"Faint-hearted"* – *ekkakeo* from *ek* (1537), out of, or an intensifier, and *kakós* (2556), bad. To turn out to be a coward, to lose one's courage. In the New Testament generally, to be fainthearted, to faint or despond in view of trial, difficulty.[93]
    - *"Proper"* or due – *idios* meaning "proper" in the sense of the individual as opposed to the general public – thus it appears that Paul is making a statement here about a personal benefit.
    - *"Time"* – *kairos*
- Two words exist for "time."
  - *Chronos* – a period of measured time, from which we get "chronograph" or a timepiece. Chronologically, Jesus arrived between 4 and 2 BC.
  - *Kairos* – the idea of a specific time of accomplishing something. But in conjunction with the *chronos* time, Jesus arrived

---

[92] Young, R. (1997). *Young's Literal Translation* (Ga 6:9). Bellingham, WA: Logos Bible Software.
[93] Zodhiates, *The complete word study dictionary: New Testament.*

at the proper *Kairos* time – the exact time for accomplishing his mission as Messiah.

- For example, when the demons beg Jesus not to destroy them (Matt. 8:29), they ask, "*Have you come here to torment us before that time?*" There was a specific time they were looking for.
- In Luke 12:56, Jesus accuses the Pharisees of being able to "*discern the face of the sky and the earth, but how is it you do not discern this time?*"

o Many other examples of *Kairos*, including in verse 10 where it is translated as an "*opportunity.*"

- Grow faint – *ekluo*, to loose out of or to grow weary.

o In other words, as believers, we can be certain that there *is* a proper time when we shall enjoy the fruits of our labor. We should not necessarily assume that this time is while we are still on earth, but we know that it will certainly be when we are united with Christ.

➤ Paul concludes this with a final exhortation to believers:

- Therefore – because we can be certain that 1) a man reaps what he sows and 2) we will receive our reward at the proper time
- As mentioned, the opportunity here is "the appointed time."
- Do good works toward everyone, and especially towards those of the household of faith, the church.

Galatians 6:11-15

11 Ye see how large a letter I have written unto you with mine own hand. 12 As many as desire to make a fair shew in the flesh, they constrain you to be circumcised; only lest they should suffer persecution for the cross of Christ. 13 For neither they themselves who are circumcised keep the law; but desire to have you circumcised, that they may glory in your flesh. 14 But God forbid that I should glory, save in the cross of our Lord Jesus Christ, by whom the world is crucified unto me, and I unto the world. 15 For in Christ Jesus neither circumcision availeth any thing, nor uncircumcision, but a new creature.

➤ If there was any doubt about who the author of Galatians is, Paul clears it up here.

- It was not uncommon for people in Paul's time to use a secretary, or amanuensis. Nevertheless, Paul has taken over here and is writing the concluding remarks personally.

- There is speculation that Paul writes with large letters because his own eyesight was poor or because his hands had been damaged by numerous beatings. However, there is no real evidence to support that theory.

- It is equally likely that Paul is writing with large letters to show the change of scribe, highlighting the different style for those in the congregation reading the letter.

- Paul may also be writing in these large letters to give emphasis to the conclusion, much the way we might capitalize words or phrases today.

➤ Now Paul makes a final push to encourage the Galatians to abandon the foolishness of the Judaizers.

- What's the motivation of the Judaizers?
  - To make a good showing in the flesh – in the Greek, to be good-looking or pleasant in appearance
  - To avoid the persecution of the cross
  - To boast about those whom they caused to become circumcised
- Once again, he reminds the Galatians that the Judaizers do not really obey the Law despite wanting the Gentiles to be circumcised. In essence, the Judaizers were afraid of peer pressure, of what their fellow Jews might think of them.
- If there's a take-away for us in this passage, it is to beware of doing things so that we present a pleasant appearance to the world, ignoring the truth of Scripture or watering down what God's Word says. This is essentially what most mainline denominations are doing today. Sure, we can make an argument that what Paul wrote just doesn't apply to us today because it's a different time, a different culture. But if God's Word is timeless (and that's a "since," not a hypothetical!), then what Paul wrote then has been preserved for us down through time and is as applicable today as it was then.

> Rather than boast in his accomplishments, Paul would only boast in the cross of Christ.
  - Through the cross, the world is crucified to Paul and Paul is crucified to the world.
    - The word for "*world*" is *kosmos*, which can mean the world, but also the universe.
  - Recall that Paul had said back in Galatians 2:19-20 that he had died to the law and been crucified with Christ.

- What are you boasting in? Are you boasting in the things you do? in your job? in your wealth? in your skill at something? Paul didn't do that. He was walking in the Spirit. When we do that, we boast in Christ's work in and through us. When we walk in the flesh, we boast in our accomplishments.

- He concludes by reminding the Galatians that when we are in Christ, it doesn't matter whether we circumcised or not. Our physical appearance doesn't matter to Jesus. It doesn't change our status in this age of Grace.
  - Paul said much the same thing in 2 Corinthians 5:17: *"Therefore if any man be in Christ, he is a new creature: old things are passed away; behold, all things are become new."*
  - You are already a new creation! Perhaps not a perfect one, but you are becoming one through the process of sanctification.

 Galatians 6:16-18

> *16 And as many as walk according to this rule, peace be on them, and mercy, and upon the Israel of God. 17 From henceforth let no man trouble me: for I bear in my body the marks of the Lord Jesus. 18 Brethren, the grace of our Lord Jesus Christ be with your spirit. Amen.*
>
> *Unto the Galatians written from Rome.*

> Finally, we come to the end of the letter and Paul's closing blessing to the Galatians.
  - He offers both peace and mercy to those who follow *"this rule."* But to which rule is he referring?
    - *"Rule"* here is *kanon* in the Greek—something straight that is used a measuring rod/stick.

- It only makes sense to back up to see if we can find a *"rule"* or "yardstick" to be measured. I think we find it right in the previous verse where Paul is talking about being a new creation. In other words, anyone within the congregation who adopts Paul's correct teaching about salvation through grace versus the Judaizers' position on requiring circumcision is to whom Paul offers this blessing. Likewise, there is an implied condemnation to those who do *not* follow in this rule.

- There is another group here that is blessed – the Israel of God.
  - This is the only time the phrase is used in the New Testament and its meaning has generated much debate. Who exactly is *"the Israel of God"*?
  - Some translations, including the NIV, remove the connecting *"and"* and replace it with a dash. In other words, they have interpreted this for you and told you that they think it is the same group as in the first part of the sentence.
  - The NLT also removes the *"and"* and simply makes a new sentence, declaring "They (those who follow the rule) are the new people of God." This is an egregious error, taking liberties with the text and pushing replacement theology.
  - The Message is just as bad (as it is in most things) – "All who walk by this standard are the true Israel of God – his chosen people." Eugene Petersen presumes not only to equate the first group as the true Israel, but also to tell you that this group (and not Israel as the traditional nation) are God's chosen people. Nowhere is this in the original language.
  - Basically, then, there are two perspectives that we see here.
    - As in the choices made by the translators in the versions above, Paul has renamed the church as the Israel of God.

- Paul is actually referring to his people, unbelieving Israel.
  - ✓ There appears to be no good reason to take the first position. Paul's other writings, in particular Romans, shows Paul's constant concern for his people. See Romans 11:1-2: *"I say then, Hath God cast away his people? God forbid. For I am also an Israelite, of the seed of Abraham, of the tribe of Benjamin. God hath not cast away his people which he foreknew."*
  - ✓ The New American Commentary makes an excellent point:" it is strange that if Paul intended simply to equate the Gentile believers with the people of Israel that he would make this crucial identification here at the end of his letter and not in the main body where he developed at length his argument for justification by faith."[94] If Paul were going to introduce this new concept – the replacement of Israel by the church – why not provide us with an explanation? He certainly has spent a good deal of time in the letter up to now explaining every other position he's taken.
  - ✓ I think it makes sense simply to see this as a remembrance of his people and a request for mercy upon the nation that is still lost.
  - ✓ The Bible Knowledge Commentary states:

    (The NIV errs in translation **even to the Israel of God** rather than "and upon the Israel of God" as in the NASB) While some believe that "Israel of God" is the church, the evidence does not support

---

94 George, T. (1994). *Galatians* (Vol. 30, p. 440). Nashville: Broadman & Holman Publishers.

such a conclusion. First, the repetition of the preposition ("upon" or "to") indicates two groups are in view. Second, all the 65 other occurrences of the term "Israel" in the New Testament refer to Jews. It would thus be strange for Paul to use "Israel" here to mean Gentile Christians. Third, Paul elsewhere referred to two kinds of Israelites—believing Jews and unbelieving Jews (cf. Rom. 9:6). Lest it be thought that Paul is anti-Semitic, he demonstrated by means of this benediction his deep love and concern for true Israel, that is, Jews who had come to Christ.[95]

- ♦ Note – I disagree with the last sentence. I think Paul clearly shows his love and concern for *all* of Israel and, in particular, for those Jews who *had not* yet believed in Christ.
- ○ Why spend so much time on this? Because it's a great example of how a bad Bible translation can completely change your theology for the worse by introducing the bias of the translators. When in doubt, stick to the KJV and the associated underlying Greek translation. And if you haven't done a study on the differences between the Textus Receptus and the so-called Critical Text, I would urge you to undertake one.
- ○ Note also that believers coming from a Reformed perspective will almost automatically assume that Paul is talking about the church as the Israel of God.

➤ Paul inserts a comment in Galatians 6:17 which seems a little out of place – *"From henceforth let no man trouble me: for I bear in my body the marks of the Lord Jesus."*

---

95 Campbell, *Galatians*, 604.

- The marks he refers to in Greek are *stigmata*, a word we probably recognize as more common in the Catholic faith as an outward sign where a believer is afflicted with the marks of Jesus' crucifixion. Literally, it is to puncture or to brand.
  - St. Francis of Assisi in 1224 is the first recorded claimant of displaying stigmata. According to Wikipedia:

    > St. Francis of Assisi is the first recorded stigmatic in Christian history. In 1224, two years before his death, he embarked on a journey to Mount La Verna for a forty-day fast. One morning near the feast of the Exaltation of the Cross, a six-winged angel reportedly appeared to Francis while he prayed. As the angel approached, Francis could see that the angel was crucified. He was humbled by the sight, and his heart was filled with elation joined by pain and suffering. When the angel departed, Francis was purportedly left with wounds in his hands, feet, and side as if caused by the same lance that pierced Christ's side. The image of nails immediately appeared in his hands and feet, and the wound in his side often seeped blood. In traditional artistic depictions of the incident, Francis is accompanied by a Franciscan brother.[96]

- But to whom is he referring? The Galatians themselves or the Judaizers?
  - He is perhaps reverting back to the early part of the letter where he claimed his authority as an apostle and is reminding the Galatians of that.
  - He might also be contrasting these marks on his body from the many beatings he had endured to the mark of circumcision that the Judaizers bragged in. Remember, Paul said he would brag only in the cross.

---

96 Wikipedia. (2018, Sept. 22). Stigmata. Retrieved from https://en.wikipedia.org/wiki/Stigmata

- ➤ Finally, he concludes the letter as he began it – with the blessing of grace to the believers in Galatia.
    - Note that there are no personal greetings or mentions of anyone in the church as we see in other letters.
    - There's almost a business-like aspect to the closure – short and sweet – as though he's finished a difficult task in writing to them and is relieved to be done.

CONCLUSION

- ➤ We have finally finished the book of Galatians, one of the most significant doctrinal letters of Paul. It's been a struggle at times to work our way through Paul's various arguments in order to understand exactly to whom he was speaking at which points.

- ➤ But stepping back, the message Paul was sending was clear – Grace is the better way. Against this, the Law cannot stand. We don't need outward physical displays of our belief like circumcision; God doesn't want that or care about it. Rather our outward display should be the fruit of the Spirit, particularly towards our fellow believers with whom we are to share our burdens.

EPILOGUE

We have concluded the book of Galatians! It may have taken longer than you expected, but hopefully, that's because you led a robust discussion. What do we need to take away from Galatians? Simply put: Grace is so much better than Law. Whenever you are feeling legalistic or are tempted to judge others because they are not living up to your standards, remember Galatians. As a Christian, you are free to live a life unencumbered by rules and regulations. Christ died to set you free from the Law. Never, ever put yourself back under a set of rules you can never keep and are ultimately meaningless, and don't let your church, your friends, or your family put that burden on you either! Enjoy your freedom in Christ but do it responsibly.

--LMA
2019

DISPENSATIONAL
QUICKPRINT

Dispensational Publishing House is striving to become the go-to source for Bible-based materials from the dispensational perspective.

Our goal is to provide high-quality doctrinal and worldview resources that make dispensational theology accessible to people at all levels of understanding.

Visit our blog regularly to read informative articles from both known and new writers.

And please let us know how we can better serve you.

Dispensational Publishing House, Inc.
PO Box 3181
Taos, NM 87571

Call us toll free 844-321-4202

www.DispensationalPublishing.com

www.ingramcontent.com/pod-product-compliance
Lightning Source LLC
Chambersburg PA
CBHW052135110526
44591CB00012B/1727